Is Death So Good That Life Is Bad?

Ralph Lee, Jr.

iUniverse, Inc.
New York   Bloomington

Is Death So Good That Life Is Bad?

Copyright © 2010 Ralph Lee, Jr.

iUniverse books may be ordered through booksellers or by contacting:

iUniverse
1663 Liberty Drive
Bloomington, IN 47403
www.iuniverse.com
1-800-Authors (1-800-288-4677)

ISBN: 978-0-595-46252-0 (pbk)
ISBN: 978-0-595-90552-2 (ebk)

Printed in the United States of America

iUniverse rev. date: 03/8/2010

INTRODUCTION

I can remember sitting in a psychology class at the University of Tennessee at Knoxville in 1998 and reading a poem written by some anonymous writer. That poem struck me powerfully; it was short, simple, and to the point:

> First I was dying to finish high school and start college.
> And then I was dying to finish college and start working.
> And then I was dying to marry and have children.
> And then I was dying for my children to grow old enough
> for school so I could return to work.
> And then I was dying to retire.
> And now, I am dying . . . and suddenly I realize
> I forgot to live.

How tragic for this person, I thought. Right then, my mind was fixed. I would not allow the same travesty that befell the anonymous writer to happen to me. My life would be full of exciting adventures and meaningful finds.

Then I graduated from college, got a job, got married and did what I thought I was supposed to do. It was important for me to set up my insurance, 401k and retirement plan to ensure the stability of my future. But there was the nagging question: Why? Why ensure the future? In an attempt to answer the nagging question, I made a grand discovery. I discovered that while trampling through the rose garden I neglected the aroma of the rose. There I stood, snared by the trappings of time and structure. Within the structure of the "normal," I had become the person in the poem, always stuck in either yesterday or tomorrow or both. Realizing my prison existence that I had developed through mindless obedience to the norm, I picked the locks of my shackles and broke free from my bondage.

I am writing this book because *now* is the time. Initially, I had been waiting to get my masters degree, but that has yet to materialize. I was waiting until I got discovered for my quick wit and philosophical savvy. Nope, not yet. I would first wow the airways via a talk show or some stupendous feat of psychological unfolding before writing the book. But that had not happened. I was waiting to get older. Then I began waiting to get smarter. I waited for revelation. Guess what? All of that waiting is wrong. I am writing this book because *now* is the time.

My studies have brought me to the logical conclusion that to avoid *now*, for any reason, would be to life's demise. Oh, how clear this point became while at an Erykah Badu concert. There was a particular juncture when Erykah decided to just play one deep, vibrant, consistent, base beat for a long period of time. (BOOM- BOOM-BOOM-BOOM-BOOM) The beat intruded on my internal organs, which bounced to the pound of this beat. I closed my eyes and tried to assess what I felt. I realized it was not all my internal organs that bounced to the beat; it was just my heart. It pounded louder than anything, internal or external. With my eyes closed and my heart beating to the base beat, I realized that I was being reintroduced to life. I am alive — not just alive, but I am alive — *right now*. Every day we swing to the routines of living, habituated. We wake from sleep and go to sleep so that we can wake from sleep to go to sleep all over again. And whatever makes the loudest noise becomes most important. Bills, cheating spouses, successful children, wayward children, first loves, possible riches, possible failures, unexpected catastrophes, religions, jobs and such all fight for center stage until we actually call them "life." But at the moment Erykah was playing this one base beat. (BOOM - BOOM) And this beat burst through the foundation of my past and shredded the blueprints of my future. I am alive, right now.

Our lives are under siege. The tyranny of the past, future, socialization, religions, and family mandates are placing us in harm's way. It appears the entire world is pressed to conform, to lose life's nectar, the *now*. Even so, I must concede that I have no desire to separate anyone from her friends, family, past, future or religion. But I would exhort everyone to consciously consider each of these *now*.

For whatever reason, I have been allowed behind enemy lines. I have infiltrated the opposition's planning staff and looked at the blueprint designed to sift from each one of us the precious gift of life. Yet more gratifying to me than the viewing of this intent, however, is making it back to affirm knowledge of how to disarm these tools of threats to life. I can live life unencumbered and show you how to live this way as well.

Until about fifteen years ago, I lived a dangerous life. I would lie with the ease of taking my next breath. Or, as a darkie, I would dawn the door of known dimwits who still believed in racial superiority, so I could ravish their daughters to see what the end would be. More than once I have received death threats. I didn't care. Hell, my trigger finger was just as fast as anyone else's. For curiosity's sake, I would frequent areas known to be less than safe and wholesome. On every occasion I wanted to challenge the boundaries of both the conventional and the forbidden, endlessly searching for something.

But I must not paint a misleading picture. Despite my dangerous lifestyle, I was not the guy that you would avoid on the street. Nor was my background one of controversy and turmoil. As a matter of fact, I appeared quite the opposite. I was blessed with two wonderfully loving parents and three amazing siblings who, at the drop of a hat, would do anything for me. And my resume of personal qualities was not bad either. I was charismatic, smart, popular, athletic, tall, dark and handsome. And, oh yeah, I was stubborn, confident, right all of the time, judgmental, competitive and extremely persistent. I had experienced both public and private schools. I was versed in the dual language of white talk and black talk, which in my day was an essential skill. My favorite talent was making people feel comfortable. All the while, I was looking for something.

Well, the something that I was looking for, I have found. For a long time everything that I was involved in seemed empty and useless. From my religion to the divorce of my first wife, it all meant "whatever." High school and college was such a blur that I questioned their relevance. I was good athletically, but the awards I received didn't inspire the same hardiness that other athletes seemed to enjoy. I was a powerful speaker. But my speaking career collapsed as my worldview changed. The conclusion was simple: everything was futile.

While in the midst of questioning living, I questioned my life. I was taught, "weeping may endure for a night, but joy comes in the morning." I can remember ministers compelling a young me to "be encouraged, for soon this mortal will put on immortality, and there will be a new heaven and a new earth." Basically, the message that I learned was that it got good when you got dead. Hence the question: Is death so good that life is bad? Is it? My immediate answer to this question was, "Absolutely not." But why not? Maybe death was better than life. No, surely life is better than death. But, why? Over the course of many years, I have come to grips with why I believe life is better than death. I would like to, in the chapters that follow, show you how to answer this question conclusively for yourself.

If you are wondering why you should bother to answer the question, "Is death so good that life is bad?" I will tell you. To invest thought in this question is to create a sturdy foundation for life-or-death choices. When you seriously undertake the challenge of answering this question for yourself, you will evaluate who you are, apart from the mandates placed on you by outside forces. We have allowed the constructs of living to dilute life. Answering this question will act as a filter, purging the impurities from your day-to-day routine. I have to admit, when I first entertained this question, it was only superficial; however, when I began to drill through the hurt of being me, new questions that needed answers would arise. Each answer to each question vaporized my need to fit into a mold created by this world and allowed me the liberty to be myself. Why should you answer the question, "Is death so good that life is bad?" You should answer this question to discover who you are.

Now that you know why you should answer the question, you need to know how. To answer the question conclusively, you must first come to grips with several issues: What is your definition of death? How do you define life? Are you constantly absorbed in your past? Is the thought of your future overwhelmingly stifling? Do you think your own thoughts or what you have been taught to think by your religion, society, or family? What does *now* mean to you? Does *now* simply organize yesterday and prepare for tomorrow? Do you know what you want to do? I pose these questions to shake you from the routine thinking that has come to prevail in our community. Images bombard us daily, telling us what life should be and what death is. Constantly, religions and cultural ideologies blast us with standards of what good and bad are supposed to be. The cycle continues, reaching to the masses from generation to generation. To answer the question, "Is death so good that life is bad" for yourself, you are going to have to step away from the preached word, social pressures, and family persuasion. Now, I am by no means saying that you should disregard all of these, but, rather, see them as separate from yourself, not as yourself. You see, it is time for you to become responsible for yourself, not insulating yourself from others but knowing the difference between them and you. How do you answer the questions Is Death So Good That Life Is Bad; you identify whether you are dead or alive.

What happens after the question is answered? You grow your greatness. I am extremely excited about growing your greatness. When we grow our greatness, we become the combustion for the next person to become the combustion for the next person to become the combustion . . . When you are aware of whether or not you are dead or alive, you will then be in position to realize your greatness. No longer will you meander around in the state of just existing. Your being will emanate purpose. You become the catalyst of the world. I look for conversations to tell people that the world could not exist without them. In a day when we are trying to find out where we come from and where we are going, I think it is time to consider where we are. However beautiful a picture your designed future may be, you will never get there without *now*. And as putrid a painting as your past may be, you are here, not there. After you answer the question Is Death So Good That Life Is Bad, you will know that *now* is what you have to work with. You will be eager to power the world with *you* and not some watered-down, communal-laden, I'm-telling-you-what-you-should-be version of you.

The flow of the chapters that follow will start with a time in my life and the lessons that I have learned. I have come to full conviction that we are all totally composed of all of our yester-moments. With this knowledge in mind, I will allow you into my yester-moments by way of illustrating ailing or troubling questions. Religion is a big subject in my life. As you read through some of my yester-moments, you may feel compelled to lay the book aside and retire to the pleasant comfort of life, or what is considered life, as you have known it. I ask that you give me a shot and read my challenges and opinions. Also, death can be a sore subject that has been poorly discussed in our society. I will try to break the walls of this bleak, desolate, sideshow and speak to the real issues. I am in no way intending to be insensitive to anyone's lost loved ones; however, I will not accept excuses for not facing the big question. Finally, you will have a challenge at the end of each chapter, and only you hold the answer key. Only you know what is right and wrong for you. You just have to look.

By the conclusion of the book, I expect change in you. I have thought long and hard about what life and death are to me. I have seen the inadequacies overrule my life and create a cycle of birthed ignorance reigning supreme in my existence. By addressing the issues of this book, you can avoid the pitfalls of this cyclic ignorance chain. Some of you have allowed the wife or husband or partner that did you wrong to sensationalize the imperfections of men or women, thus swearing to the tainted nature of all men or women. And some have sworn off all relationships. There are some of you who have gotten financially strapped and see no end in sight. Others of you feel that you have disciplined yourself to get what you've got, and that is that, but you're not happy. I don't pretend to know the cure to cancer or how to turn stone into gold. I am not going to try to prove the Creation Theory or Evolution Theory. I am not going to promise you heaven, enlightenment, karmic release, or any religious stuff that we hear and talk about. I will, however, show you that you can make it in this world. If you shed the weight of the past and the future, you will see what needs to be done *now*. Your finances, health, job, spirituality, religion, social status, emotional state, relationship, and any other thing that is involved in being you will improve should you follow the teachings of this book.

I have heard that life is what you make it. I have also heard that we have been predestined to fail or be great. I have heard that life is what it is. The answer lies within you. You are right. You know what needs to happen to make you whole. Humanity has been laden with excuses for too long. No longer will you rely on the excuse that your quality of life is someone else's fault. It is time for you to pick up what belongs to you and make it happen. Thank you for coming this far in this reading. Keep reading and watch your greatness grow.

DEATH

There are many schools of thought on the subject of death — so many that the world community is geographically sectioned off according to what it thinks of death. You can map it. Eastern philosophy, for example, speaks primarily of reincarnation, the continuation of the soul in the wash weary and tumble-dry cycle of death and rebirth existence. The process of reincarnation cleanses the soul of bad karma so it can successfully reach *moksha*, liberation from this cycle of death and rebirth. Another consideration is the western thought, Christianity. This philosophy of death is your ragtag, Cinderella wear, will magically, and in a twinkling of an eye be changed into ball apparel. Consider also the sporadic scatterings across the globe of the scientific, or atheistic, point of view: one dress, one wear, and that's it. And, of course, don't forget the rare sightings of an endangered species, the agnostic or no knowledge vantage point, standing in a full closet with no idea of what to wear. Discussion could go on and on about the different concepts of death. You can argue that Plato had it right when he separated the soul from the body, as the soul continues the body rests. Or you might agree with his contemporary, Aristotle, who made the soul and the body one, and when the body died, so did the soul. You can say that the scientists are right; it's just firing synapses. You can pit Christianity against Buddhism, agnosticism against atheism, Scientology against humanism, religion against science, but to what avail? All arguments on death depend on what you believe. So in this chapter I will not try to change your belief about death; however, I ask that you think, feel and assess what you believe death is. Why do you believe what you believe about death? And, how does your belief affect you *now*?

After many nights' tossing and turning, I have come to understand death to be the continual suffocation of the possible. When I was younger, I used to believe death was when something good was taken away forever. I lost a favorite dog, Bennie, which didn't seem fair. Later, I believed what I was taught by the church; death had something to do with your soul. After a while, I just went with the general populace. He's dead, they're dead, it's dead, she's dead; I ain't dead. Or am I? I had to think about it. I had to think about what death meant to me because I had never seriously considered the subject. Have you?

Have you lost something or someone that was special to you? How did that loss make you feel? Had you ever experienced that feeling before? Does sadness, pressure or despair evoke feelings of death? Are there such things as feelings of death? Should you ever feel dead? Who told you what dead felt like? Are death feelings painful? Is it good not to feel pain? These questions have to be both asked and addressed in order to answer the question *Is Death So Good That Life Is Bad*.

The assumption that death is always a bad thing has permeated the American culture. The bad of this assumptive notion is that death hurts. Much has been written about the proper way of ridding your life of pain, suffering and heartache. Some people tell you to put on a happy face. If you only think positive thoughts, then you will only encounter positive actions. The bulk of your community has been duped into believing that there is some good life out there that is devoid of struggle, and you're left with the bad life. This thinking is, literally, a death sentence. Life is sustained by a natural, living process. When you interrupt the living process, you jump-start the dying process. It took me a while. But I had to just stop. I had to stop running from all possible pain, suffering and heartache because to avoid these warning signals is to avoid growth. Then you die. Our community routinely tries to numb itself from pain, struggle, and heartache. And the antidote to pain is as deadly as our neglect of the warning signals that we are trying to numb. Religion convinces many to focus on the future, and that's a nail in the coffin. Social structures are demanding focus on the future, and that's one foot in the grave. Self-loathing is whispering, "Correct your past," and that's just digging a six-foot ditch. You are being taught that the extremes are normal; that you can be happy all of the time or that you are eternally doomed. This is just dirt tossing. When you avoid defining death - when you negate the possible, you cover yourself in a six -foot mound of dirt. It's suicide. I should know, because I tried it. Thank God, I failed.

The only way I knew of physical death was via association. Neighbors would tell me the grim details. When I first began writing this book I had not known physical loss first hand, and without that, all of my theories of loss were perverted. My best attempt at consoling others was, "God knows best." I was full of emotional detachment, intellectual verbiage, and insistence that life went on. Then loss came my way. It was swift, final, and totally unexpected.

I was ready to get married a second time, and her family and I was a match made from the heavens. I especially enjoyed the company of dad. We did not use the term *in-law* in our relationship. It was simply *son, mom, dad, sister,* and I longed to call Towanna my wife. One day while on the job, I received a call. The voice was exuberant and energetic.

"Hey son, why don't you meet me at the house in a little while for a game of Play Station?"

"Hey dad, I would really like to, but I have to work late today," I declined. "Can we do it later tonight?"

"No, I have got the class tonight and have to be up tomorrow for a meeting. That's ok," he said, "We will get together tomorrow."

I stayed at work and did my thing. I left work tired and not feeling up to much. My mind was made up. I was staying in tonight. But I received a call from my fiancé. She was insistent that we go to dad's Ti-aerobics class.

"Precious," I said, "I don't really feel like it tonight."

"Honey," she insisted, "I think we should go."

"Ok," I surrendered, and we went to dad's Ti-aerobics class.

Dad was in tip-top shape, for all appearances, a young man who ate well, worked out constantly, and connected with his spiritual self every chance he had. But that night, in front of his two daughters, a son-in-law-to-be, and fifty or so of his students, he fell to his physical end in a massive heart attack. I cannot begin to articulate how my wife and sister felt. The man that has always been in their lives was suddenly no more, right before their eyes. Mom would typically be with him in class, but that night she had another engagement. Soon the police were escorting her into the hospital.

"I am sorry, Mrs. Stone. We . . ."

The unfathomable had happened: Dad was dead. Surreal does not begin to describe the feeling. I could not process this event intellectually. I could not get a grip on my emotions. What could I say, do, or for that matter, where could I go and hide? All those who dad had affected all of their lives were at a sudden loss. What would be the outcome of their lives? Now I am not just talking about the immediate family, but a whole community; who all seemed to be at the hospital now. What role did I play? Play, play, play, Oh, my God! I should have gone to play with dad today. I wondered if he knew that this would be the last opportunity for us to talk. Was there something that he wanted to tell me? Why did he call? Why did he want to play in the middle of the day? Why didn't I just go? Why did Towanna insist on us coming tonight? Am I supposed to be doing something right now? Who is going to look after the family? What would dad do at this time? Wow, my wife is hurt. I have promised to take her hurt away. I don't know how this hurt came to be. What should I feel? I am confused.

Towanna and I left the hospital to gather some clothes to stay with mom. I knew that I had to call mama and daddy, my parents. So, I called.

Hello daddy," I said. "Daddy Rick is dead."

"What?"exclaimed my father, "I'll be right there," though he lived an hour and a half away.

We all stood together now: confused, shocked, and dismayed. I had three beautiful, talented, and strong women whose eyes seemed to ask me, "What do we do?" Or did they? I only know for certain that I did not have the answer. Mom asked me to handle the funeral. Prior to taking the pulpit I cried, and I rarely cry. I simply did not understand. We made it through the ceremonies, and it has been an uphill battle for the family ever since. But in the wake of a shocker that topped the Richter scales remained three beautiful, talented, and strong women who held their own.

I had to assess what happened. What did the loss of this man who had accomplished great things mean to me? I had to go beyond the questions of why this happened and was God trying to tell me something? Dad was such a good man; why not take some of these sleaze-balls from around here? Is it fair? Was it my fault? Could I have done differently? Am I going to drop dead tomorrow? Who's next? How will I go on? Can I go on? What would the loss of this great man mean to me?

I settled in and thought only of dad. From the first day I met him, he was at peace right were he was. Now, don't think that I am merely trying to be respectful of one who has passed on. That is not it. This man actually was at peace with where he was. He could have hung his hat on the fact that he started a business from the ground up that fortified a community. He could have rested on his accomplishments in karate alone, achieving the highest honor that could be awarded. His family was enviable. He was a man of discipline, drive, intelligence, and resolve. He was an instructor, protector, provider and spiritual leader. He was at peace with where he was. What does it mean to me, the loss of this heroic man? Nothing.

Before you judge me for being too harsh, let me explain. There has been no loss. Peace cannot dissolve. A person lifted from the depths of despair, even briefly, cannot dismiss the reality of being lifted. Every time I saw dad, whether in deliberation over a problem or casually bouncing along in play, he was good. Right before he fell to his physical end on stage, he had jumped down from the stage and bounced around the room, encouraging all of us to keep up the good work. He would stand next to a person having trouble with the steps or keeping up with the music and march them through the routine. He was smiling broadly and doing his thing. Then his body stopped. But, to me, he never died.

When I say that dad never died, I am not talking about death in the traditional sense: his spirit going to rest, recuperate, or receive rewards. Nor am I trying to say that his spirit remains here with his remembered acts. I can't conclusively prove either option anyway. But I can say with conviction that dad did what he could with what he had. Dad explored all of his possibilities. Not one of us has an excuse to hang our hat on that justifies neglecting the possible.

My intimate experience with physical loss taught me that I could not simply dismiss death as a general concept. Death is bigger than that. And now that I have shared my yester-moment with you, I would like you to ask yourself a few questions to clarify what death means to you. Take your time with each of these questions. You don't have to show anyone your answers. I suggest that you do them alone. In a time when we need a support group for everything, some things are still best done alone. Also, while answering these questions, search deeply and see where the answers come from. Are they teachings from your particular religion? Are they what your parents or family members have told you since you could remember? Did you learn them from a television program, get it from a university, or is this what you have come up with on your own? Be careful now, these lines of influence are shady. Lines of influence are very hard to distinguish sometimes. Take your time. Contemplate who you are and what you believe.

1) What do you believe death is? (All aspects of death — physical, psychological etc. . . .)
2) Based on what you believe death is, how does your belief affect you now? (Is there something that you have to do in order to secure a good or bad death?)
3) Where did you get your belief of what death is? (Social or religious influence or on your own?)
4) How did you come to your conclusion about death? (Mandates from outside pressures or no?)
5) Are you affected emotionally or intellectually by your definition of death?
6) Based on your answer to question 5, how does the loss of loved ones or things affect you and why?
7) Do you prepare more for death or life?
8) Death of a stranger: What does that mean to you? (Be sure to insert your definition of death.)
9) Is death permanent?
10) Is death fair?

11) Do you have a universal definition of death for yourself? (Death of an animal, flower, or insect: Is death the same for these?)

When I first began trying to assess what I believed death was, I came across an interesting point. I had never actually considered death; I would think about the cause of death, and then I would think about post death, but never death itself. When someone is dead, what does that mean to me? OK, it means I will never see them again, speak with them again, talk or touch them again, be able to confide in them, cry on their shoulder, be directed by them, argue with them, fight them, or do anything consistent with interaction ever again. On the other hand, should I die, I would be in a state of rest, waiting for the glory train of body change to come and take me home. This was my thinking on death. Does it make sense to you? Well, I'd say that I have yet to deal with death.

When one is dead, the mechanics of the living organism ceases to function. But one could be dead psychologically, existing only in a vegetative state. Let's say that one's social life is dead, devoid of interaction with people. Each of these examples suggests that death has something to do with stopping; to cease.

My church, of Christian philosophy, taught me that death was physical. But Christianity also asserts that if you accept Christ, you will live forever. Then Christianity tells me that if I did not accept Christ I would be punished forever. Well, according to this logic, 1) death can't be physical, and 2) I won't die or cease either way. Eastern philosophy tells me that if I did not get my karma right this go around, I will get another shot. So what is death?

I know for sure that I cannot prove whether I am going to go to heaven or not. I also know that I cannot prove that I will be able to cleanse my soul. What I do know is that I have the opportunity to either embrace the possible or neglect the possible. Should I not take this chance to do what I can, I am dead to the chance. Success in anything is not possible if I neglect making an attempt to achieve my goal. The crux of it all is that I will not immediately recognize my demise. Demise comes slowly. Death became clear to me when I accepted it as a process rather than a one-time event.

I used to believe that death was when my body stopped, and then an uncertain fate would commence contingent upon how well I lived this life. That is to say, if I accepted Christ and followed the teachings of the church, then I would live in heaven forever. But should I go astray, I would reap eternal damnation. That was death. This philosophy of mine came from the religion that I was brought up in. This, my homegrown church philosophy, did not answer my questions. With questions unanswered, I then believed that death was solely physical. So if I ate right and exercised, I would live forever. I would escape death with modern technology and proper diet. The only way to die would be to stop taking care of myself physically. I grew past that. Life had to be more than chronological accumulation. Then I fell hard into the psychology and philosophy of living vs. dying. I could argue for days on end about the "what ifs" and "why nots" and all that these questions could lead to. Then my eyes were opened. A baseball bat of reality beat me atop my head and told me to look around. As I looked around, I saw my talents were put up on a shelf. Literally, I had stopped playing my musical instruments. The swagger I had possessed was lost. Hope in the possible was absent. Instead, I was walking around in the, oh-woe-is-me part of my past, and the oh-my-God-no part of my future. This is what death is: not taking advantage of everything that you are and hating yourself for it.

Now, if you have dimly defined death, you are in for a treat when reality comes a-knocking. And if you are just going along with the social teachings of death and have never addressed the issue for yourself, that lack of knowledge will affect you. The world community seems to see our existence as an organizer of the last moment and a steppingstone to the next moment. The substance of what you are involved in now has little to no value — until tomorrow, of course. Tomorrow you will look back on today and ask why you did not use your talents. What is your immediate significance? If everything that you do today were to cease, would there be significant repercussions? Can you just stop?

Tomorrow is a vision. Tomorrow is a hope of things to come. Tomorrow is death waiting to happen. Tomorrow is a conception that cannot be proved. Death is constantly investing in yesterday or tomorrow so you lose the very best that you have available to you, *now*. When paralyzed by the refusal to let go of the past and mesmerized by the uncertainty of the future, dying begins. Dying is the process that concludes in death. If you are not aware of the process, then you cannot circumvent the inevitable.

An overdose of structure, routine, habits and conventional thinking is poisonous. You are being poisoned with the concept that yesterday and tomorrow are more important than today. You have been ingesting this deadly attitude daily. You say you are stuck in the rat race and back to the grind, the belief that you can only do what your society allows you to do. You are stuck. You can see it in the way you eat. Instead of enjoying the fork full of food, you are busy considering your next fork full, dying to die. And you begin poisoning your kids with death. You are so proud if your kids walk, talk or read faster than the other kids. After you get the children to say da-da, you rush them to ma-ma and so on, dying for your kids to die.

Why is it done this way? It is because there is a belief that the next moment is better than this moment. Or you believe the improvement of the last moment will induce birth to a better next moment. I had the privilege on several different occasions to sit in with some kids of our family and watch them open Christmas gifts. I was amazed that at every sitting the same thing happened. Instead of the children enjoying the gift in hand, they were more excited about the next gift. Not three minutes after a little girl opened one of her gifts, I asked her what she thought of the last gift. She had no idea what she had received. She had just ripped off the wrapping paper, said thank you and then went onto the next present. After being questioned about her opened gifts, she took a second look.   When she went back to inspect what was beneath the wrapping, it was a new ball game. We grownups can be like these kids with their Christmas gifts. Take a moment, look beneath the wrappings to find the treasures you have, instead of constantly considering what awaits. We seem to perceive the imaginary possibilities of tomorrow as having greater luster than the opportunities of today. We also seem to give more value to what was than to what is. To slow the family down, my mom would use the adage, "always preparing and never prepared." I have finally taken heed of mama's wisdom. What I have is now. And I will use what I have or I will begin to die.

Two years after dad died at age forty-nine, my daddy died at age fifty-six. I could not believe it. My father, whom we called pap-paw, was the most darling man. Pap-paw had patience rarely seen in this world. I had read about his kind of patience in books, like historically great leaders of nations or spiritual prophets, pap-paw would confound the naysayer with his wisdom and ability to weigh the hostility with unwavering hope in a productive outcome. Pap-paw was that dude who made everyone his best friend. I loved hearing his voice. Even more than that, I loved seeing his smile. He would transform a room when he entered. He was a large man with a presence that commanded attention. He was quiet when needed to be and outspoken when he needed to be. Sometimes daddy would consider the opinions of others; sometimes he wouldn't. But whichever way he went, it was because he chose it. Daddy was a great man.

One day out of the blue, pap-paw contracted leukemia. Call me stupid, but I didn't know that you could catch cancer. For four months he was in the hospital. I saw my daddy go from a 250-pound man with a head full of neatly groomed hair to a 190-pound, bald man.

Pap-paw would visit the sick and attend a hurting family in the wake of a loss. He was the resident mechanic, fix-it man, financial advisor and daddy-come-quickly-I-cut-my-finger man, always on the move. Now he was confined to a hospital bed for four months. My daddy was also a pastor. On Sunday mornings, whether he had a church full or just the family, he was going to preach. He lived free and unencumbered, until he got sick. He was a private man, and now people were coming into his hospital room when he was in a state of undress. He had always stood proud with shoulders back. But he started to look sickly. He was dying, right? Nope, not pap-paw.

I showed up at the hospital every chance I got. To my surprise, and then again not really, daddy would be having church in the hospital. Nurses from his floor and surrounding floors would congregate in his room, along with other patients and members from churches around the community, to have church. One day during a visit, daddy said, "Let's walk around." Do you know what he did? He visited all of the sick that he could, prayed for them and told them it would be all right. They would come from all over to see big Ralph. Pap-paw did not shy away or act different in any way. He would smile big and make all that came to see him feel better.

I sat in the hospital one day with my mom and pap-paw. Pap-paw was out of it. My mom looked at me and said, "He is not doing well." I could not contain myself. I sat in the chair and just cried. I could not hold back the tears. I wanted to fix whatever was going on with my daddy. I did not want him to die. When I saw him the next day, I asked, "How are you doing pap-paw?" He gave this huge smile and said, "I'm a'ight." It was at that point that I remembered. Daddy was not concerned with what he did or did not do yesterday. Neither did he take much thought in what was going to happen tomorrow. Pap-paw had what he had, so he did what he could do with what he had. While daddy was on a respirator in the ICU ward, my mom was told that it was over. Daddy was dead. It has been an uphill journey from that time to now. To tell you that my mom and siblings are strong would not do them justice. We have all inherited from pap-paw something that can't be driven away: life. What did the loss of this great man mean to me? Nothing. There has been no loss.

Through experiences past and appreciation of the work that I am doing now, I understand that I have a choice to live or die. I weighed the benefits of each to see what would be best for me. I asked myself the question, would I rather be dead or would I rather be alive? The answer was easy, especially after the absence of dad and pap-paw. In good times or bad, dad and pap-paw, took what they had and dealt with it. My mind is made up. I want to be like them, alive and well. What about you?

IS DEATH SO GOOD THAT LIFE IS BAD:

(Song written for pap-paw's funeral)
Thinkin 'bout DADDY

Chorus
I'm just sittin here thinking bout daddy;
Bigger than life to me.
He walked dat walk; the one he talked;
And he grinned incessantly.
He was a man on a mission;
His works and deeds you could see
And I know he affected others;
Because he affected me.

1st Verse
Working long days and long nights, standing up to the test.
A worker in his community, striving to do his best.
Tired sometimes, weary and worn, love was always sown,
With the spirit of God inside him, it was the spirit of God, shown.

2nd Verse
A preacher and a pastor, husband and father too.
He'd visit the sick and council his children.
He did what he could do.
Neglecting his health, he kept on pushing himself;
His hand he'd always lend.
Still the greatest thing about my daddy,
Was my daddy was my best friend.

(Chorus)

Break
But it ain't over.
My daddy's in a better place, he's done finished his course, he's done run his race.
But it ain't over.
I see him walkin down the streets of gold, were his story's been written, read and his story's been told.
But it ain't over.
God said welcome son, you were faithful of few; well done – well done – well done.
But it ain't over.

My daddy's in a better place.
But it ain't over.
My daddy's in a better place.
But it ain't over.
My daddy's in a better place
I'm just sittin here thinking bout daddy, bigger than life to me...

PAST

The one-way bridge we call the past stretches from your birth until the ticking clock of now. No matter your desire, financial standing, relationships, political connections or religion, you can't go back. What was is what was. Despite that fact, there remains an air of insistence that the past can be redone. I'm sorry. The past can serve as a steppingstone, a learning tool, a reminder, and an inspiration, but it can't be repeated.

Your past is vital. You are the sum total of every moment of your existence. Nothing is lost. Everything that you have been involved in is available for your use. And you should use it. Look at your past as the blueprint of your present. Take your past and analyze it until you come to full understanding. But don't get sucked into some hopeless consideration of trying to go back and right some wrong. It ain't going to happen.

The past will never change. Yet droves of people are spending the bulk of their time trying to undo what can't be undone. The language from generation to generation continues to recycle the idea of undoing by barking idioms like, "If I could only turn back the hands of time," or, "If I only knew then what I know now." Well, you can't and you didn't. Yet the thoughts remain. If I had not hit him, if I had not missed that meeting, if I had been there before the crash or if I had not quit the team, then life would be different. This kind of thinking is suspect. It first presupposes that your present existence will be improved if you could only change your past. This is a supposition that cannot be substantiated. You don't know if it will be better or worse. The idea of changing your past distracts you from now. It is one thing to have thoughts of redirection, but to mull over the impossible is futile. The repercussions of continuing to try to undo the undoable, is massive destruction on the *doing*. Put simply, remaining in a constant state of looking back disallows you from seeing where you are.

Here is the self-righteous question: Why do people keep trying to do the impossible? The past is not some magic key for unlocking the door to utopia. Neither is the past an angry monster, trying to sift away your tranquility. So why try the impossible? I'll tell you why. Laced in your past actions are associations of responsibility or irresponsibility. You are being judged now based on your past character. Now, instead of seeing the past solely as moments gone by, you view it as people's judgment of who you are and who you will become. Consequently, you embrace the idea that if you could just change your yesterday, you could change your tomorrow; therefore, correcting the past has come to rank as higher priority than exploring *now*. And this philosophy enjoys a formidable supporting cast. Social teachings and other influential persuasions present a woeful life ever after, should you neglect to contemplate all that you have done: "Little Johnny, go up to your room and think about what you've done until I tell you that you can come down." The past has been branded as the reminder belt. The leathery whip of the past snaps at any hopeful glimpse of free expression loosed from the weight of yesterday. Try to apply for a job without supplying a resume, and see how far you get. Try to cast your vote for the presidency with a criminal record: won't count. In the game of life you are accepted or rejected by prestigious clubs based on where you come from. That's why humanity keeps trying to do the impossible. That's why you tend to highlight the good of your past and get rid of, hide, fix, or deny the bad; if you weren't worthy yesterday, then surely to god you understand that you are not worthy today. Is this mindset fair? Do you want to be judged by what you did? Do you judge others based on what they've done? Should every person's life resume be public domain? You must answer these questions. And, one of the most important questions that you need to answer is, should you concern yourself with people's perception of who you were or concentrate on who you are? What will be more productive for you, to mull over the impossible or to get on with what you've got? Rest assured that if your choice is to mull over the impossible, I won't help you much. But if you want to get on with what you've got, let's take your past out for a spin and see what it can do.

DEALING WITH WHAT HAPPENED

When considering the past, memory is an imperfect source of reference. You have to revisit the sights, sounds, smells and surroundings. However, while revisiting you cannot revert back to the character of old but rather you have to return to the old sites with new insight. With new insight, a collection of data points from experience -judgment – conviction, you deal with what happened. First and foremost, see the past as it was. Too often we see the past through the goggles of today's emotions, intellect, and social conditioning. Such a vision will never provide accurate information but rather a mere distortion of today's emotions, intellect and socialization. But peering through the goggles of detachment will reveal clearly what was. Detachment is, by definition, unbiased, as if one views from the vantage point of a separate, impartial observer. Since you are part of your past, not separate from it, learn instead to view it in an unbiased manner. What *was* is what *was*. I will hammer that home; what *was* is what *was*. Your wife divorced you. You drank to excess. You were fired. You spent your savings on alcohol. You did not graduate. This is how one man's past would look through the goggles of detachment: no drama and no judgment, just the facts. Deal with the known. Don't infer, suspect, deduce, intuit or any other variation of perception. Just deal with what happened.

I insist on this practice, and the common response is, "It is easier said than done." After investing twenty or so years in trying to do the impossible, how does the doubter make a 180-degree change of habit and say, "I'm just going to get on with what I've got"? And that's a fair question. The answer is acceptance and analysis.

Let's start with acceptance. Acceptance generates healing, enables analysis, and inspires the now. How can you accept? Acceptance requires faith. You simply have to believe that you cannot undo the undoable. There is no amount of logic or reason that can convince one who is overcome by regret that he cannot go back and make it right. So drop both logic and reason and just believe that what *was* is what *was*. It does not matter that you squandered all of your life's savings. So what if you've been married four times or ran out on all of your "illegitimate" kids. It is important that you couple with these booming events, the other stuff. Remember that you once started saving your money. You were accepted as worthy marrying material on four different occasions. You were there to father the babies. It happened. Don't neglect or deny it. Accept it, and your strength will be renewed. Accepting all of your past will actually de-gloom your today. Instead of looping around in the cycle of "coulda, woulda, shoulda," you will begin seeing the possibilities of now. Your newfound faith will provide enough comfort so you can analyze the past instead of trying to redo it. Suddenly you find yourself with a wonderful mix of believing, knowing, and health, which bakes the biggest cake of inspiration. Your being will radiate confidence. Your every step will spring with experience and belief. You can get on with what you've got if you first accept what was.

I had the fortunate opportunity to interview a young man by the name of David Rice. At birth, David was diagnosed with Cerebral Palsy. For the first three years of David's life he was told that he would not be able to walk; ever. David, now 21 years of age, can be seen stomping around campus – with the help of his crutches – bounding from class to class. During the interview I asked David if his condition was preventable. In his explanation he said that due to him being born premature there were certain physiological developments that deemed his diagnosis unavoidable. I asked him if he was angry about his condition. David would not allow me to continue the thought or trap him with the concept of regret. He insisted that he could not do anything about his prognosis. He had Cerebral Palsy and that was that. I would jab "but what if you did not have it." His responses were quick and full of conviction, "it is what it is." David said to me pointedly, "I have accepted my condition. Also, if I had not accepted my condition I would not be able to progress as I have." What do you mean, I asked. David responded, "if I had not accepted my condition then I would constantly be looking back at what could have been and not consider what I can do." All I could say at this point was, AMEN. I reiterate to you, you can get on with what you've got if you first accept what was.

THE PAST IS A LEARNING TOOL

When you accept what was and analyze the past, you equip yourself with a tool of higher education. While a definition falls short when it tries to explain something by telling what it is not, it may help you to understand that your past is not a chain that binds you to the mandate of every similar past. If you are born into a bad situation, it does not mean that you will die in a bad situation. Your past does not denounce or announce anything. You are not shackled to any learning deficiencies because you were not born into a Harvard family. Your past is your experiences. Or put another way, your past is your science project. You are a study of yourself. With every living moment, you have the opportunity to sit as an analyst and a client of study. You can peer into the vast wonders of every experience you've had, the result of which only enhances you by providing you with leverage to make more informed choices, now.

There is not one assignment that is not cultured or tailor-made for you. It is not unkind to say that this applies even to the most horrific, brutalizing, disgusting past of all times. A family member who you see daily could have dealt you such abuse that you feel earned them a bullet in the head. Yet you remain. The good thing about the past is that what was is what was. You are no longer there. And now you are privy to the learning from all of your past incidents. I'm speaking of the emotions, physical qualities, sights, sounds, people, environment, smells and attitudes. These characters of your past are communicators to the synapses of your brain. The neurons, capped with receptacle feelers, respond and transfer these characters to your central nervous system of now and demand a choice. You choose what happens next.

It is your past. You can either retake the course or make changes that promote you to the next course level.

Stop trying to delete your past. If you take anything that ever happened in your life away, you would cease to exist; you would die. What you know now is a direct reflection of what you have done before. The common mistake, when assessing the past, is condensing the past into one culminating event. The most euphoric or disturbing event becomes the memory of choice. More often than not, you will remember the time, day, and atmosphere of the car being repossessed, while you completely forget how you often neglected to pay the note. Crib notes of your past only provide information on one portion of an incident. You have to study it all. When retested on the same incident, you fail miserably. Why? Because you did not study your past. Instead, you studied a fabrication of the mind. Your past is the learning tool. To detract from your past would diminish your learning potential.

<yester-moment>

It took me ten years to graduate from a four-year institution. I attended several schools to get a four-year degree. During this ten-year stint, I had four different mindsets for the use of the schools. For the first three years I played or was involved with football. The next three years I was ultra religious. (I fought with all of my philosophy and religious studies professors. I let them know I would not embrace any notions that might jeopardize my relationship with my God.) After being ultra religious I spent three years in confusion. Is there a God? Should I be fighting the black cause or the human cause? Is any of this worthwhile? Then I took a year to graduate. I tell you this because my undergraduate scholastic endeavors where much more than book studies. I was unaware of this fact, however; I'd had a problem at the start of my undergraduate studies. Then I realized that I learned people, cultures, and most of all, me. This realization of the tools made available to me did not come until I took a good look at everything that was.

Take a peek at this list:

- I did not want to be called another dumb black jock. (My mom did not want that either.)
- In high school I was kicked off the basketball team because of my grades; even though my grades were good enough to stay on the team.
- I had lied to all of my ex-classmates about my progress in school.
- The grapevine said that my high school basketball coach thought I would never graduate from college and would simply be a thug.

- The general consensus from everyone I hung around with was that I was extremely smart.
- I did not know why I was in school.
- I had little direction.
- I challenged the traditional, even though I was a traditionalist.
- I believed the notion that anybody spending ten years to get a four-year degree had to be slow.
- I believed that it really mattered how people perceived me.

These are just a few items that swirled around my head when asked about my undergraduate stint in college. I was embarrassed that it took me so long. But rather than seeing the entire picture, I would only be embarrassed about the highlights. My considerations were how I stacked up with others. After my initial embarrassment, I started counting the people who have no degrees at all. It made me feel better that I had endured to earn a degree. Then I questioned myself again: Do I need the misfortunes of others to inflate my ego? Is my worth contingent on others' worth? No. I had to work out some things while in college. It took me ten years to get my degree. It is what it is. Or, I should say, it was what it was. My past and now and your past and now make up who we are. You can't add or take away from mine and I can't add or take away from yours.

Your past is set. There are no winds of change that will magically erase what was for you. There is no time travel to help you make corrections in your past living experiences. You just have to accept that what was is what was. But know that where you were does not mandate your now choices. You are not enslaved by your past. If you want, you can speak another language, move to another country, get a new job or work for yourself. The past does not stop you. As a matter of fact, the past is inspiration in a bottle. When you look to see where you are and where you were, it suggests what you want. It also shows you how to fulfill your desires. Many people say that the future is wrapped in the past. I don't agree. Your past is the foundation for now. How will you use it? Will you use your past to build a pit and bury yourself? Will you set your past on fire and allow the smoke to screen you from any reconsideration of where you are and what you've got? Your past is a tool for your benefit. What will you do with it?

IS DEATH SO GOOD THAT LIFE IS BAD? (QUIZ)

1) Take a moment and write down how your past can be beneficial to you. Explore how your past can help you, in the present, -spiritually, socially, physically, psychologically and financially.

_____

_____

_____

_____

_____

_____

_____

_____

_____

_____

_____

_____

_____

_____

_____

_____

_____

_____

_____

_____

_____

_____

_____

_____

_____

THE FUTURE

Time is a concept that came relatively easily to me. I learned quickly that when the little hand was on a number and the big hand was on the 12, it was something o'clock. Rather astutely, I understood that if it is 12:00 p.m. now, 11:59 a.m. has already been. I got it. No problem. These times are measurable. Along with measures, I can make associations with what I was doing, where I was. But 12:01 has yet to come. There is no point of reference or tangible item of measure for a non-existent moment. If I had to write a definition of the future as it related to time, I would write, "It is not." And, quite frankly, I am offended at the idea of the future being associated with the substance of time. The future fits into several categories, but time is not one of them. For example, the future could be a science, so you could call it a hypothesis. The future could be a philosophy, so you could call it a theoretical aberration. But the future is not time. More adequately than either of these, the future sounds like a religion.

Religion purports a principle based on faith that should be sought with thoughtful commitment. Have you subscribed to the belief that the future is time? Do you run around voicing concerns like, "I'm running out of time," or "If only there were more time," or "Time is on my side"? Why do you do that? Are you referring to the moment in which you stand? Or are you referring to the time that has already lapsed? I doubt it. You are probably relating these notions to mental concepts of hopeful or dreadful speculations. Despite the non-existence of future time, however, you believe that it will be. You invest considered effort in sustaining faith in these ideas, and that sounds like a religion to me. This religion is spoken in every language and taught in every household worldwide. The future has established itself as the only true universal religion operating in the world today. The teaching of this religion inspires both genius and stupidity. And every other existing philosophy is a subsidiary of this religion, the future. Christianity asserts that if you believe in my God, I will ensure financial blessings forever, i.e., a mansion and streets of gold. Scientists argue that if you will just look at the facts, then you would rid yourself of these idiotic notions of mysticism. Eastern philosophies contend that if you center yourself, you will have peace in your next life. People around the world say, I don't know what I believe now, but I will soon come to full knowledge. All of this smacks of the religion, the future. Is there anything wrong with traveling this path? No. But recognize the path on which you travel is one of faith, not supported by scientific evidence. There are no guarantees the next moment will happen for any of us. If the big bang theory is correct, then who's not to say the next moment could be a big bang? Or if the creation theory is correct who's not to say that the great creator genius that came up with the idea is not to take it away? I can only conclude that the future is not. Not only is the future not, but also it will never be. The only way you can realize your tomorrow is by existing in the morrow, which is your today. You will never exist in the next moment because of your permanent residence in the present moment. The world community has become so saturated in the concept of tomorrow that even questioning the next moment seems preposterous. Let it go. The next moment is a belief, and that's all.

All religions must be sustained by what its followers contribute. So it is with the future. Tithes are required. Investments of emotion, intellect, physical, and money are planned for the future. The constituents of the future preach fear. Although their holy writ does not specify, the teaching says to worry about not being prepared for tomorrow. Don't you dare get caught with your house unfinished. And if you can't be frightened into giving of yourself for the future, you are coerced by the mild-mannered voice of reason. Reason says that if people won't help you now, you know they won't help you later. And you had better start exercising. You need to take all the vitamins that you can because you have to live longer in order to fit everything in that you want to do later. Speaking from experience, should you not have stocks options, 401k, and retirement in place, people will question whether or not you are a responsible adult. It was also brought to my attention that the reason you work is so you can live the same at retirement at age fifty-five, well fifty-eight, or sixty. And if you are already retired, then cut back on your spending today, so you can live the same way tomorrow. And if that means little to you, then at least do it for your grandchildren. Thus, you are pressured daily to live a myth, encouraged to work for tomorrow, think about tomorrow, purchase insurance for the surviving spouse of tomorrow and, by all means, take care of the children of tomorrow because the children are our future. *Not.* The future is not.

POTENTIAL

Although the future is not, you still believe that this thing that is not will come into being. You believe in the potential. Pondering the potential involves three concepts: power in the possible, assigning values of good or bad to the potential, and your belief. You are taught to invest hope in the potential. So are others all around you. A poor man says, "I am going to be rich." A smart woman says, "I will solve the world's hunger problem." Two depressed kids declare they will each commit suicide. The rich say they will give to the poor. The east says "we will get revenge on the west." Such scenarios are countless. And thus hope is invested in the possibility that the nonexistent could come into existence. Do you realize what you are hoping for and how that is affecting you now?

Whether you consider yourself a risk-taker or not, you do push for the potential. You say it's your weakness, your Achilles heel. You readily admit that there is a certain allure that prompts your impulse. But are you aware of what that force is? It is the power of the possible. Take, for example, the lottery. The lottery is a multi-billion dollar industry not because it's a fun game to play but because it provides the possibility of winning. Hollywood, Manhattan, and South Beach draw huge numbers of *wanna-be* actors who hope for the potential of being discovered as the next great celebrity. The potential bates us all with such subtle manipulation. You can almost hear the silent whisper constantly chanting that all will be well tomorrow or the haunting echo howling that nothing will ever work out for you. Despite the message you receive, the possible is potent. The *potent*ial, an event or option not yet proven to be real, is so strong that it evokes immediate emotions. Emotions, in turn, create opportunities or barriers to obtaining the result. The little boy refuses to ask the little girl to dance for fear that she may say no. The woman who's lost all of her substance to gambling has to play one more number before she quits for good. Why? It's the power of the possible. You must understand the allure of the possible. Underestimating the allure of the possible could cause you to become a slave to it, doing things you say you don't want to do. Or, conversely, not doing things that you know you should. There is power in the possible; how is the possible affecting you?

It is completely up to you to decide which value to assign to the possible. And how do you make these character assignments? Remember the woman who lost all of her substance by gambling? The last number she played, she hit. In your eyes, was that good or bad judgment of potential? Do you have a personal checklist for assigning a good or bad value to potential? Or have you just been taught the nature of righteousness and unrighteousness? As you sit at mass, listening to the commandments of tomorrow and deciphering the concepts of the possible, how do you validate the message? Is experience your validating tool? Maybe you prefer historical events to teach of the value of tomorrow's potential. Or is it possible that you don't know whether tomorrow will be good or bad? Does the veneer of what seemed good fade to a reality of bad? What constitution do you have in place that regulates what your assignments are? I ask this because when a possibility is good, you will try it. If it is bad, you will avoid it. The little boy who neglected asking the little girl to dance decided that rejection would be worse than the possible payoff. What are you accepting as good or bad potential? How is it manipulating your course of action? Why did you not go after that job? Why did you make a particular decision? You did or did not do because the potential was perceived as either good or bad. The crux of it all, ironically, is that the potential is not even real. It is solely a product of your belief in the things to come.

The future is not. But the belief in the potential *is*. This faith is inspiring you to *be* what it is you believe you *will be*. A father tells his daughter of a young age: You are indeed the smartest little girl I know. The little girl believes her father. She believes that she is the smartest little girl ever, so she applies herself in such a manner. On the other hand, a mother tells her son of a young age: you are the dumbest ma'_ _ _ _ _ _ I know. The son does not believe her. He believes that he is smart. So he promptly goes out and sets a spaceship on the sun. Believing in the potential is a powerful tool. How do you use it?

There is not one thinking person who does not believe in the potential. Follow me if you will. Changing the future is not an option because there is no future. You don't have any control over what is not. But you do have control over what you believe. Do you believe that the potential houses for you success or failure? Or do you believe that the potential is set, that everything has been predestined? Do you believe in a combination of the two ideas? It is your faith that determines your intent.

Take a few moments and answer some questions:

1) Do you worry more about tomorrow, yesterday or today?
2) Considering your definition of death, would it be ok to be dead right now?
3) Do you believe living will be better tomorrow?
4) Is your emotional state predicated on possible events to come? (I.e., winning the lottery, finding a mate, getting a job, graduating, what others will say about you, etc.)
5) Is tomorrow so good that today is bad?
6) Is tomorrow such a concern that today is an afterthought?

This is not some trick. I am not trying to convince you to believe that you can speak into existence anything that is not. I don't want you to think that I am trying to get you to believe that if you think that there are no troubles there won't be any — not at all. You have highs and lows in your life. Problems arise that must be dealt with. Without your own belief, you struggle to find solutions. You can't get started because belief inspires action, and you don't even know what you believe. Others may teach you their beliefs, but if they are not truly your own, the solutions available in that framework may not work for you; you don't even believe they can.

What you believe will happen actually inspires what you do. Do you remember the turn of the century? In 1999 there were many predictions that the world as we knew it would cease. The computer systems were going to crash, Jesus was coming back, and terror was going to reign supreme in the streets of the States. A stampede of concerned Americans rushed to the banks to withdraw all of their money, emptied the grocery stores and gathered in churches for prayer because they believed in the potential. Every American who has ever worked legitimately has paid into the Social Security fund. There has not been much outcry about paying Social Security, either, because of its potential. Millions of dollars are spent annually on insurance because of the potential of sickness, accidents or theft. You do what you do because you believe in the possibility of what will be. Under the guise of being proactive, you become a willing inmate to potential's demands. Some people believe that the rich are going to get richer and the poor, poorer; that it's not what you know, it's who you know that gets you ahead in the world; or that nothing ever changes. If these idioms are true, then what of the *potent*-ial? You believe in the potential. Even if you decide that you are just going to lie curled up in bed as if you are in the safety of your mother's belly, you are making the statement that something that is not will be. What do you believe?

Sustained only by the bread and water of maybe, you travel the path designated by someone or something else. You believe in the potential. My question to you is what of the potential do you believe? Hear me when I say that I am not asking you to change your belief. But you should know for certain that it is *your* belief.

GOALS

After contemplating the idea of no future, you may ask the question: What, then, are goals? Are goals irrelevant, fictitious, and misleading in accordance with this no-future idea? To the contrary, goals are not only relevant but necessary. Goals are not fiction but discernable truth. And goals are neither misleading nor leading. A goal is cold and stationary. A goal is a designated end pursuant to a path traveled, not to be confused with potential or intent. Goals don't extend any feelings of euphoria, inspiration, or commitment. Neither is it the job of a goal to design paths to travel in order to reach a desired end. Goals are simply your own creations, choices that structure active intentions, which where inspired by the belief in the potential. On occasion I go to a local track to run. Each time around the track I notice the painted markings that say 200m or finish line. Because of my starting point and designated end, these markings have no relevance to my physical intention. In other words, they are not goals of mine. As I jog past these markings they don't inspire me, comfort me or support my endeavor. You see, these markings, in and of themselves, are nothing but painted symbols on an asphalt pavement. But after I have traveled the distance that I have deemed appropriate and come to that section of the unmarked track that I've set as my goal, hallelujah! The unmarked track is my designated end pursuant to my path traveled. My goal has been obtained.

Goals evolve from a simple formula. Belief in the potential + contemplative intention + active intention = GOAL. Apply this formula to every moment of your being. Do you know what you get? You get: every action is a goal reached. Take a second and investigate your past. How have you interpreted *goals*? Are you one who has only defined goals as those lofty accomplishments identifiable by others? Well, according to the formula, either becoming President of the United States of America or reading the next word in this sentence is all the same: a goal. According to the formula, you govern every action that you perform.

Take this one example and dissect it according to the parts of the goal formula:

Belief in the potential+contemplative intention+active intention= GOAL

Example: You are sitting in your favorite chair watching television. There is a knock on the door. You can either answer the door or not. You choose to answer the door. Answering the door requires getting up from your chair, walking over to the door, and opening the door.

Belief in the potential:
    I can either answer the door or not.
    I can answer the door.
    I can get up from this chair.
    I can walk.
    I can open the door.
Contemplative Intention:
    I will answer the door.

I will get up from this chair.

I will walk.

I will open the door.

Active Intention:

I get up from the chair.

I walk to the door.

I open the door.

Goals:

Answering the door.

Getting up from the chair.

Walking.

Opening.

Belief in the potential is faith that what is *not* will *be*. Contemplative intention, evoked by belief in the potential, is a completed goal visualized. Active Intention is the path by which you go about accomplishing what you have visualized. A goal is simply a designated end pursuant to a path traveled. You achieve goals every moment. What do you believe? What can you see? What are you trying to do?

Your goals can be simple or complex. The simple goals are quite often dismissed as normal activity. These normal activities don't require thought or much consideration. Walking, talking, speaking, hearing, touching, and smelling are unrecognized simple goals, until you can't do them of course. The complex goals stretch everything you know about you and make you grow. A complex goal challenges your faith in the potential. The pixels of your contemplative intention's images are fewer and farther apart, producing a fuzzy picture. You have multiple paths to travel with a complex goal. The success ratio of making your designated end is smaller.

Goals are mandates for you. You achieve goals every moment. Inspired by what you believe, encouraged by what you see for yourself, goaded by the actions that you take, you accomplish goals. Whether they are good or bad, you decide. There is no future. But the potential is available. And the potential is, just like the past, a tool for you to use. Designate your end. And if that end is an easy accomplishment, ok. Know that it is what you desire to do. If your end is complex, then work on your faith, make clear your vision, pick your path and do your thing. But don't ever allow a concept of time that will never be to deter you from traveling the path to your goals. You can't return to your yesterday, and tomorrow does not exist. You've got what you've got. Get on with it.

IS DEATH SO GOOD THAT LIFE IS BAD? (ASSIGNMENT)

1) I dare you to take the next 20 minutes and write down every hope that you have for yourself that you can think of without variations within the 20 minute time limit.

2) The following 15 minutes, I dare you to write down activities that you can do to come closer to achieving these hopes.

3) I dare you to take the following 10 minutes to set goals for you to accomplish within the next 24hours from the previously listed activities.

4) I dare you to take 15 minutes to think on this writing of yours and just believe in your abilities and that your hopes for yourself can come true.

SOCIALIZATION

I love organization. Admittedly, I am a little anal . . . well, truth be told, a lot anal. Organization rids your life of undue stresses. When you come into the house, put your keys in the key glass on top of the refrigerator. This eliminates the craziness of walking out the door in a frenzy, and then asking the irritating question, "where are my keys?" Put the remote back in the same place every time and avoid running around the house looking for the remote. Order reigns when you stay within the parameters of regulation. When the light is red, stop. When the light is green, go. Don't walk when the sign says, "Don't walk." Walk, when the sign says "walk." I get frustrated with disorder. If I am driving down the street in the 90 mph lane, your 45 mph driving self should not be there. Move over! And don't look at me crazy when I finally get past you because you know that you're in the wrong. Every society has developed rules that promote the smooth flow of communication. The rhythm and beat of a society is reflected as law. When the right notes are played, harmony. But, play the wrong notes and chaos ensues. Right?

I am no fan of rushing to the dictionary for someone else's meanings to define my thinking and writing. But as I researched this chapter, I ran across three intriguing definitions for socialization. *The American Heritage Dictionary of the English Language*, fourth edition, says that socialization is "to make fit for companionship with others; make sociable," "to convert or adapt to the needs of a society," and finally "to place under government or group ownership or control." Is this not interesting? These three definitions not only seem congruent, but also appear to pose an agenda. First, we get you hitched comfortably, next we see how useful you are, and then we own you. Is that what social order is all about?

Intellect insists that without order, chaos will ensue. What if you had a car traveling northbound in a southbound lane? A head-on collision is probable. Right? You have to agree with the logic. And it just makes sense to wear your seat belts because, if you were in that southbound car at the time when the northbound driver struck you head on, the seatbelts would give you a better chance of survival; furthermore, if you don't speed, then you will see an oncoming car earlier and be able to avoid a collision, so it is a good law of averages to drive a certain speed. Lower speeds help you to conserve fuel and save money anyway. It's better for the environment, too: Burning gas pollutes the air, so let's take cars off the road or at least reduce them by doing our part and car-pooling. Otherwise, we are not going to be able to breathe in the year 2030. Global warming will have taken affect by then, and the world will be destroyed. Lord, you'd best start praying now. Pray for our nation because we are all going to hell in a hand basket. I'll tell you what I think: We should legislate who should and should not have access to oil. Oil is the cause of all of this nonsense anyway. If we get those people who have the oil, then we can control the cars, factories and economy. We won't have to worry about that idiot traveling northbound in the southbound lane because he won't have a car. So there: no chaos because order is restored. Right?

This chapter about socialization may drip with sarcasm, but, um, you know, we just do what we do to get you to look the, uh, other way, or maybe to see the other way — our way or maybe their way. Socialization is about . . . (what was it?) . . . social harmony . . . that's it. Yeah, that's it. Socialization just wants everyone to be happy. That's all we are going to talk about in this chapter: what socialization is. What do you think it is? Is socialization just a big smoke screen for evildoers to hide and do their dirty work? Is it a natural, evolved animal which has turned on humanity for its sustenance? Or is it all good with socialization, and are the rebels the real problem? Is it true that if we would all just stay within the matrix, then the balance would remain constant? What is socialization? And why must we talk about it now?

Socialization has many meanings. I call it *influence*. While in undergraduate studies I had a host of classes that taught about the learning curve of babies versus adults. A child's lack of contemplative boundaries allows great leaps in learning. The reasoning behind such a notion is that a child explores everything innocently, without preconceived notions. The fear of nonexistence or the concept of tomorrow is foreign to a child. With blissful abandon, a child will climb into a dangerous pit to feast her curiosity on all that is new. The way I see it, if it is

attractive, a child's

Curiosity is piqued. Following curiosity comes

Contemplation. Contemplation evokes

research, which inevitably leads to

Understanding. The overall

experience helps each individual child to

accrue the foundational traits of what his or her world is.

When you see a child experiencing some new prize for the first time, her face reveals satisfaction, reward. The child explores the prize and finds knowledge. Then faster than a speeding thought of individuality, stronger than a moment of clarity, enters (fanfare with French horns) THE INFLUENCER. The more experienced personnel are inspired to respond to the children's accrual: That was cute, but you shouldn't do this or that. That was good, but maybe you should add this or that. I know you're safe, but it is possible that this or that (terrible or favorable eventuality) could happen. Thus influenced, in short order children begin seeking approval instead of accrual. No, I am not saying that you should neglect protecting your children from impending danger. I am not saying that imposing your perceived notions of right and wrong onto your children is bad. To be quite honest, I am trying to show that influences are neither good nor bad. Influences, if allowed, simply affect responses. And, for our communities, only certain responses are collectively considered appropriate.

In order to understand the bipartisan nature of influence, first understand what influence involves. On the surface an influencer is simply a person, place, or thing that imposes its attitudes and affects a person, place, or thing. Dig more deeply, and questions arise: What influences me? Why am I influenced, and how am I influenced? Now you must consider whether you are not only being influenced but are also one who is influenc*ing*. How and why do you influence? How does it happen? The only way to answer such questions is to strip away the body of influence layer by layer to discover the molecular make-up.

INFLUENCE

Unimpeded by concern for the future and fear of death, children innocently accrue knowledge. You knew the feeling of being attracted to something that stirred your curiosity. Contemplation of that curiosity demanded that you research with abandon for more information. Your understanding grew while your experience quenched your curiosity; you were satisfied. This cycle of attraction to experience played out over and over and over and over again. Things began revealing their similarities. Then, seemingly from nowhere, appeared a new mode of operation. Assumptions substituted for curiosity. Once the initial attraction occurred, preservation overruled spontaneity. You were no longer curious about the elements that might be detrimental to you. You just wanted the good stuff. So you went from attraction to mild interest. The next phase was contemplation. The contemplation was still there, but it was fashioned according to your agenda. Capturing the prize was no longer a study project; now you had a plan for contrived gain. Exploring everything was too time-consuming. Instead, you sought to understand only things reputed to be beneficial for you. After a while, your experiences were no longer rewarding, but diluted by concerns for what it *should* be (the future) or what it should have been (the past). You graduated from simplicity to complexity. Why? If you're looking, you'll notice that all indications point to an increased number of influences in your life. And what are influences? On the surface, they are people, places, or things, seeking to impose their will on responses.

Alcohol is a chemical blend with a distinctive smell, wide popularity, and a rep for creating change. When alcohol is ingested, a chemical fusion begins. What happens is the alcohol goes from mouth to stomach and into the small intestines where it is absorbed into the blood stream. The circulation spreads the alcohol concentration evenly throughout the entire body, and the alcohol seeks out neurotransmitters like serotonin, dopamine, and gamma-amino butyric acid and fuses with them; the drinker feels high. Gamma is an inhibitor while Serotonin and dopamine are both stimulants and inhibitors. A stimulant cranks up the system and gets it going. An inhibitor shuts it down. Alcohol connects to these neurotransmitters and cranks up some functions and turns off others. Once under the influence of alcohol, your responses change, even if ever so slightly. The more alcohol you ingest into your system, the greater the effect. (Stick with me; I'm getting there.) Consumed alcohol has, reportedly, caused inflated or deflated emotions, sluggish reaction time, and impaired judgment. I have read that if you have a .45 alcohol to blood ratio, you are dead. A .35 alcohol to blood ratio means a coma. As the alcohol to blood concentration decreases, effects are less extreme. But check this out: if you don't ingest alcohol, it has no influence at all. My point is that this is just how influences work. The more influences you absorb, the more drunk you get from the ideas of others that bombard you. Now the slightest ingestion of an influence changes your internal process. Should you consume enough, your internal process will become comatose or die.

ATTRACTION. If there is no communication between an influence and you, the influence ceases to exist. It dies. Instead of leaving communication up to chance, influencers encourage first-time meetings. Adorned with a beautiful array of delicacies, cooked specifically to your liking, influencers seek to win your attention. When school friends abandon you, an influencer offers a way to forget about them, win them back, or exact revenge. When the playing field is unbalanced, an influencer appears to offer ways to make the field even. Your family history is muddled with financial depression. But wait, says an influencer, I can give you financial freedom. No matter what your deficiencies are, an influencer will proclaim the possibilities of attainment, if only you accept the influencer. The fantastic allure makes you captive prey. The plan now is to get you engaged in conversation, during which you will be converted; first you'll feel comfort around the influencer. Then you will assume the role of ambassador for the influencer, and, finally, you will become his or her property; *American Heritage* calls this socialization. The influencer desires to convert you. The influencer believes that its aroma will entice you, and its beauty will engage you. The influencer depends on your sense of inadequacy to make you crave its strengths. As a temptress, an influencer will casually flirt with you to encourage desire. If the ploy works and you take a sip; change begins. Keep in mind that an influence is neither good nor bad. It's just getting dolled up a bit to catch your eye.

CURIOSITY and CONTEMPLATION. Whenever something catches your eye, you have a choice. Either you can accept what you see at face value, or you can inquire about it in depth. To use an old adage, all that glitters is not necessarily gold. The surface of the influencer may look and smell appealing, but it may not be what you are searching for. Earlier, I made a distinction between the research of children and the assumption of adults. The reason for the distinction was to unleash your own memories as a small child, innocently seeking to understand, oblivious to acceptance or judgment. Without question children are self absorbed and adults are laden with responsibility. The sheer nature of these two identities demands differing degrees of caution. Despite your age, however, if you're being strung along by any influence, at that point you become essentially nothing. Think. Feel. Remember: You. There are sources all around you that look good, but are they? If you need money, there are banks that could be robbed. But is that the best choice for you? You lost your wife of ten years to cancer. I'm sorry. But just because Carol looks and sounds like your deceased wife that does not mean you should put a ring on her finger. Slow down. You have all the time that this moment has to give. You can always acknowledge what is attractive at first glimpse. But before total consumption, see what's beneath the surface. Are you actually interested? Or are you just turned on by the look and smell?

RESEARCH. If you want to know if you are attracted to the whole of anything versus certain characteristics, know first what you are looking for. Once you know what you are looking for, then you can proceed on the quest.

Are you looking for a drunken, fun-filled, one-night stand? Do you want a lasting relationship? Would you prefer casual conversation right now? What do you want? When you know your needs, you can drill through the facade and get to the meat of the matter. Would money actually make you happy? Is God a figment of your imagination or a devout Catholic, Baptist, Hindu or Jew? Is your house a place you can call home? What appeals to you? Search both internally as well as externally for the answer. Clarify the distinction between what you think and what you have been told to want and need. Then research. Look at the word *re-search*. *Re* is a prefix used to indicate a need to do again. *Search* is to mull over or through. The most basic definition of re-search is "to look again." First time glances don't tell the whole story. When enticed by any substance, at the very least, look again. And, remember, you are looking again to find what *you* want.

UNDERSTANDING. Research is complete when you understand. Check out this story, one of my yester-moments. I had read so many books, talked to so many people, and was pretty confident with what I wanted to write in the pages of this book. But I found myself blocked. I could not complete a thought without questions ripping my concentration to shreds. For two weeks, this went on. Then one day I decided to call my mama, a top notch influencer of the best sort.

"Mama," I said, "I have a question for you. I have been trying to get through this book and bla bla bla bla."

Mama said, "You are going through the growing stages of the book. You were exploring all of the questions as a child does. You didn't have to give answers. But now, as the grandpa of the book, it is time to figure out what you are saying." With words of wisdom and a voice of concern, she continued "it's like traveling around in a circle and seeing, for the first time, all of the paths that you can travel to explore new adventures. But, once all of those paths have been explored, you get tired of driving, and you just want to go home. Every musical instrument has a home key. Could you imagine if there was no home key on the piano? All of music would be a crescendo, without the pleasure of a culminating end."

What a wonderful thing for my mom to say. It had taken me traveling around the states, physically and mentally, to understand that at some point you've got to make your way home. I called my mama because I knew, intrinsically, I had to go home. Understanding is bringing it on home. What if the big house on the hill is not home for you? What if the huge bank account and billboards are not home for you? What if the school out West is not home for you? What if the six-dollar-an-hour job is not home for you? And what if it is? When things come your way to try to affect your outcome, you have to ask the question, "Can this get me home?" If not, it's just a ride around the circle that leaves you dizzy with confusion. Just to quote the good book, "In all thy getting, get understanding."

EXPERIENCE. The overall experience of everything that you do informs you of the only power that influence has outside of you. That is the power to make itself attractive. Also, your experience suggests that if you allow influence in, you will change without question. Truth lies in experience. Somewhere in your past, you have seen something that had the potential to persuade you in a direction. Your mom could have said that this is the outfit that you should wear. Even with all of the positive points that your mom made, you were not deterred from your thinking that your mom's choice was wrong. Despite the force coming against you, you rejected the notion because you were not impressed with the whole packet. On the other hand, you have noticed the increased population of Mexican Americans. At one point, you made remarks that belittled any person outside of your likeness. You heard a "joke" that was completely distasteful to anyone. You internalized the feeling. You intellectualized the outcome. You considered the consequence. You changed. You realized that all people are people, deserving a chance to shine. Experience brings to the table an ability to move from the circle of confusion to the comfort of home.

Home-going is an amazing journey. The time it takes to get off of the circle of questions and confusion is relative to each person. The necessities of the trip are those flasks of influencers that we sip on from time to time. There is not one person who has not been influenced by something. It could be as simple as a favorite color to peer pressure, but there is a source that has gotten inside of you and begun a change. At some point you accepted a "truth," and then it changed. At various other points you disbelieved things which now you know to be the infallible truth. An influencer, just like alcohol, came in and both stimulated and inhibited. Remember how my mom told me that after traveling around in a circle for a while, you just want to go home? Well, socialization is the circle. You ask yourself all of these moral, spiritual, physical, political, financial and social questions, and pretty soon you just want to go home. After being on the journey for a while, amazingly, you become accustomed to the sights and sounds. After growing accustomed to these sights and sounds, you recognize that this is not my way home. Or you realize that this is my way home. Still, your end is not complete; just one road does not lead you home, and you are not sure of the exact path to travel. So you try another path, or you continue on this same path to find your doorstep. All of this searching is but to find the right grid path to home and comfort.

What ignites passionate frustration, though, is when you can see your way home but you are not doing the driving. Everyone brings their influencers along on their trips. The problem comes when you have reached a .35 influence-to-self ratio and suddenly find yourself overcome by physical appearance or other superficial issues, until you become an unidentifiable blend of mucus squashed under the shoes of impressionism. You remain inside the designated walk paths, not for safety, but because you are mindlessly wandering around, drunk on that thing that is reputed to be right for you. You are so sloppy drunk with influence that you keep your ears to the ground. You listen to see what's going on in the pop culture. You have relinquished control to others. You know what you want. You know what you feel. But you are in the passenger's seat.

Every time I turn on the television and see our pop culture promotions at work, I cringe. We are so into the herd mentality that it sickens me. If the rappers are wearing it, then Footlocker is promoting it. If Britney is doing it, then MTV is endorsing it. If Whitney and Bobby are involved in it, then the media is covering it. And we, the rest of the un-popular wanna-bees, are looking for all that we can duplicate from these pop stars, so we can be important enough to be exploited. I know it makes you angry to go to bed broke when you want prosperity. I know that it is hard being lonely when you want to be at peace. Living is difficult enough without the frustration of knowing how to get home but not being able to go. Answer this question. Do you want to drive?

I tell you what. I know that this chapter has meandered along the byways, a distinctly informal read. I know that you have questioned the direction and flow of this chapter. You have asked yourself questions about politics, socialization, family and friends. You have thought about religion, drugs and drinking. You thought about whether there was an evil intent on the part of an arbitrary "they." You questioned whether I was recommending that you adopt the meandering style of a child's thought process. I did that on purpose. You see, socialization is just another tool available for your use. You can use it to make yourself feel good, if you want to. Or you can flip the script and use socialization to make yourself feel bad. Socialization can be your neighbor or a person on the other side of the world. Socialization can be the color red or the color blue. In any case, socialization is an influencer. But it cannot be an influence to you without you.

Since you were a child exploring the new world until the present, you have been converted. We all have. Our community has become a nation of finger-pointers and excuse-makers. Are you a finger-pointer and an excuse-maker? Or do you know why you do what you do? Are you taking the time to accrue knowledge, or are you coerced into doing what is reputed to be beneficial for you? Have you been drunk for so long that you have forgotten the feeling of sobriety? Or have you been drunk for so long that you are afraid to change? Are you in denial? Whatever your state, I dare you to step away from the bottle of influence for a day, and see what you accrue. Can you tell the difference between "them" and "you"?

IS DEATH SO GOOD THAT LIFE IS BAD?
(DISCUSSION)

1) Make a list of everything you want to achieve in Life! (no restraints)

YOU CAN DO ANYTHING YOU DECIDE TO DO!

RELIGION

Oh my goodness, religion. If religion was wrong, I didn't want to be right. My God, the singing, the camaraderie, the structure, the potential and the power were so seductive. I wanted to understand the game. I wanted to feel the presence of this Magnificent Other. My taste buds longed for the sweet nectar of transcendent necking. I wanted to speak to the God in the cave, wrestle with the angel all night, get caught up in the chariots of fire, and see water coming from a rock, smitten by my hand. But, more than anything else, I wanted to be God's pick. Out of the millions, possibly billions, traveling the wide road to destruction, God would recognize me on the straight path and say, "Well done, my good and faithful servant." I would go to heaven to rest in eternal bliss. I would languish no more. My street would be of gold and my castle would be laced with the no-wear, no-tear carpentry of eternity. My perfect fruit would line my perfect street, and I would nap with the lions. I was going to heaven. And the only way to get to heaven was by way of religion. I was clear about that.

So my journey for clarity began. When I was six years old, I was sitting in the back of a large church, along with the rest of the kids. I can remember the pastor standing there emphatically encouraging us, the sometimes-listeners, to give our lives to Christ. With intermittent concentration, I was thinking that it would be a good thing to go to this place called heaven. It was appealing to me to fulfill the criteria. I did not understand all of it, but I knew that it seemed right, for the time, to take up Christ. So, in big-boy fashion at the time of the altar call, I got up and traveled down the long middle aisle. My goal was to be undeterred and make it to the pastor to shake his hand and be able to go to heaven. Out of all of those people in that building, not one other person got up, so I was really walking that aisle alone. It didn't matter though. I just wanted to go to heaven. But suddenly and to my surprise, from the offset wing of the building a big, handsome, muscular man was coming to the altar also. It was my dad. My dad did not see me coming, and I didn't see him coming either. But in simple terms, daddy wanted to go to heaven like me. It was confirmed. On the same day, in the same place, and after hearing the same message, my daddy and I accepted this dude called Christ so that we could both go to heaven.

The trip home from church that day was extremely exciting. My mom was not able to attend that day, though she was undoubtedly the spiritual leader of the house at the time. My mom was constantly trying to get all of us to go to service, so we could go to heaven, or so I thought. So, when we walked in the door and my dad told my mom that I walked that aisle like a big boy, my mom was so proud. Not only was she proud of me, but she was proud of my daddy as well. There it was: more confirmation. I was going to heaven.

From this exciting day to the next, my knowledge of what it took to go to heaven increased dramatically. My dad was a huge factor in my increased knowledge of the Christian doctrine. Every morning, and I mean every morning, my dad would call home from work before I went to school and go over a Bible passage from the book of Proverbs. I was fed on knowledge of the Bible from a very young age. From the teachings of my parents and the teaching of the church, I knew the difference between right and wrong. I was made privy to the gospel, unadulterated truth, the God-breathed word that revealed to me how I should stay out of the bad spots in order to go to heaven.

Going to heaven is not a bad thing. Would it not be wonderful to take a break from the weariness of living? Everyone gets tired, and the concept of heaven appeals to all people. Don't get caught up with semantics. You could be using the terms enlightenment, *moksha*, peace, furlough, or whatever to express rest for the weary. The point is that we all need a vacation. I have no religious dilemma at all about people wanting a "heaven." My religious dilemma came when I was convinced that I should show everyone the way to make it to their heaven.

RELIGIOUS CONVINCING

At a young age, I desired heaven. But I could not hear directly from God yet. When I informed the church officials of my problem, I was often referred to the scripture that told me I was just a kid, nursing on the milk of inexperience. I could not wrestle with the angel yet; I had to be obedient to the church first. I had to follow those who followed Christ. I did not know initially, but soon learned that the following of Christ had a hierarchy: pastor, deacon, minister, trustee, mother of the church, choir member, first lady, usher, Sunday school teacher, missionary, then the members (according to age, of course). Basically, if I had a good reputation with the church, I would then be privy to access God. If I could just talk with God, then he would guarantee me entrance into heaven.

Establishing a good reputation with the church was the beginning of my religious derailment. After accepting Christ as my personal savior, I moved from the back of the church to the front. I began studying the preachers. I would be overwhelmed by their ability to move a crowd. The deacons would present themselves as the most distinguished men in the community. And I admired these distinguished men. The women of the church would be so helpful in their positions as missionaries, teachers, and kitchen attendants. Everyone had his or her role. And, if they would do their jobs to the best of their ability, then God would be pleased with them and say, "Well done. Come to heaven." It did not matter that the women were being misused in this patriarchal community. They would just turn their cheeks. I came to understand, by way of the church, that God was not concerned so much with what you were going through in this world, as much as he was with how you handled what you were going through. So when I found myself in a fix, I would do what the church taught me to do. I would pray all day every day, visit the sick, give financially, be upright in the community, and never get caught with my work undone. I tell you what: I was doing what the church told me to do, how the church taught me to do it. Despite my obedience to the church's instruction, however, I still did not get to wrestle with that angel. But I was convinced.

My faith grew, not in God, but in my religion. I learned to love the rules of the religion game. And it just so happens that the church that I was affiliated with did not permit any unrighteousness. Women wearing pants were going to hell. If you said a curse word and Jesus found you in your un-forgiven state, you were going to hell. And forget about that once-saved, always-saved crap. If Jesus came back and you were thinking about having sex with someone outside the bonds of marriage, you were going to hell. Should you do anything outside of the rules of my religion, you were going to hell. It was that simple. I loved the structure. Loved it. I loved the church so much that I stopped listening to my parents and heard only the church. I got married so as to avoid getting caught thinking about premarital sex. I got into cahoots with some of the leaders of the community and convinced them that I should be in their "cabinet." We would make changes all around the district at will. I did not understand that we were doing this at the time. I just obediently followed the community leaders because I was taught that obedience was better than sacrifice. And my purpose behind it all was to go to heaven.

I became one of the ministers and was even allowed to pastor a little church, an awe-inspiring experience. The people were fantastic. I can remember the messages that I delivered to this beautiful group of people. My messages were frightening. Somewhere between age six and twenty-two, I was convinced to stop talking about *me* going to *heaven* and instead start talking about *you* going to *hell*. My radar for wrongdoing was so keen that I would point out to strangers walking down the street the errors of their ways, according to me. I got to the point that I would call church officials out on their errors. When I went to work, I would change the conversation because of the cursing or lewd comments. I would read the Bible in the bathroom on break and form volunteer prayer groups. I wouldn't drink a virgin strawberry daiquiri because it would look like I was sinning. I was going to heaven because I faithfully stayed within the confines of my religious rules. I was the man. I did not believe that anything or anyone could get to me, but one day someone did. Unfortunately, it was not my wife. It was the girl next door.

As a result of my inappropriate choices, those who had been my under girding disappeared. I lost the wife, the pastorate and the good reputation. Everything that I had held to be true and good since the age of six was suddenly a lie. I had distanced myself from my family. I did not have any friends outside of my church affiliations, and every other person outside of my religion was going to hell. Wow. I realized that I was now outside of my religion. That meant only one thing: *I was going to hell.*

I thought so much about heaven that I was living hell. Did I do anything wrong yesterday, and am I ok for tomorrow? That was my constant concern. If I could just make it to heaven, then all would be fine. But I had been taught that in order to go to heaven, I had to die or be removed. That meant I had to abandon living to go to heaven. I came to a crossroad marked by this question: Is the promise of heaven more important than living? "Absolutely not," was and is my unequivocal reply.

Religion purports a principle, based on faith that should be sought with thoughtful commitment. I had believed in heaven as a consequence of life. Analyze that word, con-sequence: with sequence. You live and then you get a prize. Somehow I had allowed my religion to pervert the belief in heaven as a consequence of living into belief in heaven as a substitute for living. At the age of twenty-four or twenty-five, I believed that I was going to hell, so at that point, not much mattered. I was in the world without the restraint of a religion, and my eyes were opened. I was amazed to realize that there were strip clubs, open prostitution and drugs all around in the city where I grew up. And it was not a secret. I was thunderstruck. Unbeknownst to me, there were actually people who sincerely did not believe in God, not to mention my God.

Furthermore, without the restriction of religion I came to realize that there were people who honestly felt that their God was God. I had been pummeled by a twenty-year onslaught of church influence. I had welcomed religious convincing. If the church said it, then it must be ordained of God. If the church ordered me to do something, then it was "ordered of the Lord," as the Book of Amos says. I obeyed the church slavishly, so the very religion that promised me liberation kept me in shackles. Ironically, amid my passionate attempt to go to heaven, it was the news that I was going to hell that freed me from bondage.

My eyes were opened. My perception was that religion had devoured my friends, family, and foundation. I simmered in the disdain of organize religion. I tempered my emotions with the prospect of revenge on that ravenous beast. I realized that if I was going to be the trailblazer who stamps out religious foolishness, I had to be smart in my approach. So I began to study. I stashed my emotions on the shelf and looked for the truth, and I found that the truth of the matter was that religion had done nothing to me. I had had the option to choose the path of conviction or the path of convincing. After a few steps on the path of conviction, I had realized that the path of convincing seemed easier, so I had chosen the easier way.

CONVINCING VS CONVICTION

In every moment you have the opportunity to either operate under the influence of convincing or by the inspiration of conviction. You choose. Convincing and conviction differ in four very distinct ways that yield opposite results; your choices lead either to increased influences or to enhanced identity.

The first of the four differences between convincing and conviction is the process of decision-making. Convincing requires two or more entities to make a decision. Convincing mandates that sources outside of you add substance to your choices. It is the salesman's pitch of how well the color, style, and price fits you that tip the scale of favor for purchase. Your school decision is almost certain when you add your best friend's boyfriend's dream about you walking around at that school. Those winds blowing outside of you validate your decision. Conviction, however, operates alone. Conviction processes the sources made available, wades through the multiple choices and concludes on its best path. Conviction mobilizes it's intent and goes it alone, heedless of the dreams of others, the color, style or price. Ask yourself this: are you being convinced to do what you do or are you convicted to do what you do?

The second difference between convincing and conviction is the source of inspiration. Convincing depends on outside elements to motivate action. If the stock does well, then I will invest. Or God, if you save my daddy, then I will worship you. All the inspiration that convincing has to offer is mere puppetry, a choreographed dance of "if this happens" and "then I will." Convincing only continues to inspire if things keep going your way. I believe this call-and-response relationship to be dangerous. The dependence on outside sources does not entice me. The brand of inspiration that arises from conviction, however, is self-inspired and self-sustaining. Certainly confirmations and encouragements help, but conviction bolsters an internal fire not dependent on the reflected light of external factors. The fire of conviction burns so white-hot that the only way to quench it is to ignore it; acknowledge the inspiration of your inner conviction, and great things happen. When conviction is in control, telephones, light bulbs, airplanes, computers and automobiles come into being. Conviction inspires men like Mahatma Gandhi and Dr. Martin Luther King, Jr. to say to a world community, "Despite your violence toward me, I will remain non-violent." The inspiration of conviction fortifies men like Mohamed Ali, the heavyweight champion of the world, to say, "I don't care about the title. I will not fight for an unjust cause." In several counseling sessions I have been asked how to sustain the will to do good. My answer used to be, "Pray for it." Now my unwavering advice is, "Pay attention to your conviction and beware of convincing."

The third, and vitally important, difference between convincing and conviction is the assumption of responsibility. Convincing assumes no responsibilities. None. Both the convincer and "convincee" can point one towards the other and pass blame. When someone or something convinces you to act, you can always blame them if you fail. You can relinquish your responsibilities. You didn't lose weight because the program wasn't right for you. You don't go to church because of the hypocrites there. You can't get ahead financially because the government taxes you so much. When you live your life under the influence of convincing, then you are at the mercy of the convincer. And, if the convincer is no good then there you are fat, churchless, and broke. But it ain't your fault. Conviction, on the other hand, takes full responsibility. Conviction evokes action, irrespective of consequences. The totality of conviction's action is taken under consideration at the birth of the action. For example, a man decides that he is going to come out of the closet and reveal his sexuality. Whatever becomes of this action is due to the action. All responsibility is assumed with the action. Once out of the closet there is no going back. Another interesting element of conviction's assumption of responsibility is that it is not concerned with what others think. Conviction does not loose weight because of a fad or go to church because of who is or is not there. The purity of conviction's first step fortifies conviction of whatever flak it may receive due to its choice. Conviction says that I am doing this, I know why I am doing this, and I'll take whatever that comes with it.

The fourth difference between convincing and conviction is the make-up. To convince, a persuasive case had to be built with the support of a string of case files and studies. Once the research and the mouthpiece were in place, then the agenda was launched: the desire is to influence thinking, to transform a point of view. Convincing is manipulative and persuasive. It is a composite of profiles intent on redirecting. I have a beautiful little sister who is off the chain. She will let you know in a heartbeat, "I'm not conceited, I'm convinced." Now don't even try and trip. I am not speaking badly of my little sister. But this logic says that by way of the evidence given, I have to agree with the findings that I am — whatever. The reverse, however, suggests that without the support of evidence, she must be conceited. Belief according to convincing depends on evidence. And, should the evidence waver, then so will the belief. Conviction, on the other hand, assumes an air of omniscience. Conviction does not require proof or evidence, validation or persuasion. Exploding from an internal spiritual cavern spews all knowledge about any given thing. Conviction employs your emotions, intellect, physicality, surroundings, teachings, and experiences. Conviction disregards limitation and demands success. When everything and everyone all around you says that it cannot be done, conviction says, "You can do it." Conviction does not seek approval or reason. Conviction just knows.

We need both convincing and conviction in our lives but in reasonable balance. Take a look around you. Are you hearing the world saying to you, "Operate under conviction"? Not likely. When you turn on the television, commercials are trying to convince you to buy this or that. When you go to work, your boss or co-workers are trying to convince you. In the grocery store, at the movies, our entire society has bought into the need to be convinced. So with all of this convincing around you, you need to discover conviction. Research it and learn all you can. Amidst all of this persuasion and manipulation, some source somewhere must be saying I should because I think I should. I went to church and was convinced, not because I was weak or less intelligent. I was convinced because I stopped paying attention to conviction.

My first experience with conviction was when I was six years old sitting in the back of that church, contemplating heaven. I don't remember what the Bishop was preaching about. And I have no doubt that the influence of my mom and church affiliates of times past were influential in my belief structure. Despite those influences and the other opportunities I had to show my desire to go to heaven, this was the moment. I knew it was the right thing to do. I had the choice to continue talking with my friends or making fun of the old people shouting in the front. I could also have suppressed my conviction. But I didn't. It was time for me to walk that aisle. When I walked down the aisle, I was not concerned with what anybody in that building thought of me. I did not care what the kids were going to say when I returned to my seat. I just knew that what I was doing was what I needed to do, from my own conviction. After I made it to the altar and was surprised by my dad meeting me there, I turned around, and a whole host of kids were coming down the aisle. I don't know why they were coming; it's not important anyway. But I do know that I needed my religious experience to understand the difference between convincing and conviction. My dad once told me that according to the book of Galatians, religion was just a guide to lead you to spiritual understanding. Whatever your religion, be it science, magic, walking, or exercising, it is just your tool. What are you using your religious tool to do, to awaken you to operate under conviction or to keep you convinced?

NOW

Because I exist *now*—I believe—I will exist forever more. And my *now* existence is predicated on the idea that God, the eternal, carved a section of eternity into a slice of restricted designation. We call this slice of eternity *time*. While my creator is eternal, I do not believe that I am eternal. Eternity is time-less. I believe that I have a linear existence; at a certain point in time, I was created, and from that point, I forever will be. My belief in eternity frees me from the bonds of time.

I am not trying to foist my belief on anyone. To the contrary, I would like for each of you to believe what you believe. The dilemma is not how to convert, but rather how to communicate eternity. Science requires quantifiable measures. And the short and simple truth about my belief in my forevermore existence is that I cannot prove it. Nor do I care to try. But I would like to note that the only thing that society can truly call quantifiable — is *now*. Physical end is potentially unavoidable and not measurable. The past cannot be recovered or altered, but it is measurable; potential is not measurable, but *now* is measurable; the past and the now are the only measurable values of existence; however, you can only measure the past from *now*. Thus, the only quantifiable measure of time is *now*. Substantiated in every breath that you take is the fact that you cannot consider the past or the potential without *now*.

I cannot tell you how many discussions I have had about the *now*. True to form, every discussion includes the supposed, fleeting nature of *now*. Every breath is un-retainable, according to those who oppose the *now* philosophy. The argument continues: not only can you not retain the *now*, but you can't even realize the *now*. I've been criticized with the objection that anyone who rests hope in the *now* will ultimately end in frustration. Time moves too quickly. Time is without pause. In order to isolate a moment that could even

44

be considered *now*, you would have to first anticipate the approach of *now*, coordinate *now*'s arrival and have enough patience, as you continue in time, to watch for *now*'s reaction to your encounter. Basically, your molecular structure would have to be accelerated beyond current measures of time. The molecular acceleration would permit you to watch time as if it were in slow motion. Those who oppose the *now* philosophy believe that this is the only way one could possibly live in the *now*. Those who emphatically denounce the *now* theory argue instead for the potential or the past. People who are comforted in the potential say, to believe in *now* is to stagnate, that *now* thinkers lack vision. On the other side of the pillow are those who believe in the philosophy of the past. Past thinkers place more significance on what went on, rather than what is going on. The world community has become so anaesthetized with the influence of the rising and setting sun that it is collectively confusing time designation. The consistency of the sun's rotation has caused a false sense of time, and it needs to be addressed. So, let's you and I have, yet, another discussion on *now*.

Any exhaustive discussion about the philosophy of *now* must include its two main identifying elements, the irresponsible now and the responsible now. Dissecting these two elements will properly conjugate the marriage between individual and corporate existence. Also, laced within these two elements is a misappropriation of time. It is here that I must make the distinction between projecting, remembering and being, and, finally, adaptability. Without adaptability, even paying attention to where you are will be futile to maintaining a healthy marriage between individuality and corporate existence. *Now* is the catalyst to everything that is, as far as you are concerned.

The sun has consistently run its course from east to west every day of your life. It has become so predictable that meteorologists and TV forecasters are giving you the time of morning the sun will rise in your area. And you have accepted the sunrise and sunset as a day that has come and gone in your life. Interestingly enough, the celestial sphere called the sun does not move around the Earth. There has never been an occasion when the sun rose or set. The earth revolves around the sun. It is from your perspective that time is designated. Astronomy teaches you that the easiest way to determine one rotation of the earth is to designate a spot outside of the earth as a position point. The moment you leave that point until you return again gives you the reference as to how long it takes the earth to rotate. This rotation speed sets the standard. If there are variations in the rotation, you deem the variation abnormal, different, or odd. Given all is normal, after you calculate how long it takes for the Earth to rotate, you can then see the average of how many rotations that people hang around on this planet. Once you get the average of how long people hang around on this planet, you can guesstimate how long you have left to remain on this planet. Once you guess — get that, *guess* — how long you have left, you can put your life into perspective, as compared to everyone else's life. You say, "The sun came up and the sun went down, so I have about ten more rotations ahead of me, and what have I accomplished?" Generally speaking, people express the notion that walking, talking, schooling, marriage, children, financial success, retirement and death should happen according to the number of rotations one has been on the earth. And, should you not accomplish these things by the standard rotation time, or should you accomplish them prior to the standard rotation time, then you are abnormal, different, or odd. Should a catastrophe occur prior to your self-designated allotment of time, you question the justice of the situation. Or, should someone fall pray to the hands of those with ill repute, yet they have lived beyond the measure of time that you have designated as appropriate, well hey, at least they lived a long life.

The Earth's rotation time allotment has become so technical, that you are made aware of the sub-second spin of the earth. You capture the idea of the earth's spin in little gadgets called clocks and watches. Then you monitor these timekeepers for second-hand movements and govern your daily actions accordingly. Now, despite the fact that time is designated from your perspective out instead of another's perspective in, when you are asked about *now*, you consult your watch or clock. You have allowed something that you have created to legislate your actions and responses. This is a problem, because *now* is not legislated by your clocks and watches. *Right now* is not the ticking of the seconds, of the minutes. Too often the technical calculation of the earth's rotation is brandished as the norm, the standard. You should ask yourself, "The standard of what?" You should ask yourself, "Why should I marry or work at a certain age?" Or, "Why should I have to wait until a certain time to marry or work?" Ask yourself, "Is it not my timetable to get things accomplished according to my abilities?" Go ahead. Ask yourself. Ask yourself, "Is it not from my perspective that the sun rises and the sun sets in my life?" What are you ready for? If the earth keeps on spinning, and seconds keep on ticking, and you are not ready to do whatever, so what, *now* is not the time. Flip the script. If the sub-second ticks of your timekeepers are moving too slow for you, and you are ready to take over the world, forget the earth's spin and do your thang, *now. Now* is not restricted by time.

I remember when I was eight or nine years old, and a friend of mine named Kevin showed me how to animate sketches. Kevin was known for his artistic prowess. This day, in particular, he was sitting in our kitchen drawing, like he always did. I noticed that he was drawing seemingly the same thing over and over. I asked him what he was doing. He told me to wait a few minutes, and he would show me. I watched. On several squares of cut up paper he drew the same character, with small variations, one right after the other. I noticed that the drawings were drawn in the same section of the squares, with respect to each square. After he had come to the point where he felt that he had drawn enough, he told me to watch this. He stacked each square one on top of the other. The order in which he stacked the square, I know now, was with respect to the idea that he was trying to get across. Then he told me to look at this. With one hand tightly clamped on one end of the stack of squares and the other flipping through the other end of the squares, these once inanimate characters, drawn on cut up squares of paper, came alive. I was amazed. For several weeks after Kevin's demonstration, I went on a tare trying to create my own sketch show. Seeing as I was not an artist, it was difficult. But I could make a mean stick-man animation. Anyway, what I learned in that whole ordeal was that in order to pull the animation off, I had to ensure that the sketches followed a certain sequence. The first sketch was the foundation for the animation. Each subsequent sketch had all of the characteristics of the first sketch and previous sketch, with a little more mobility. I had stick men and women jumping and running and crying and all sorts of things. I could even reverse the order. My characters could go from crying to smiling. All of this was done by the flick of one end of cut up squares of paper.

Now houses everything that you have access to. Anything that you do not have access to is only potential. *Now* houses all the essentials, like: your five senses, intellect, emotions, experiences, family, culture, social permissions, genetic makeup, the outlawed, and belief. Think through this simple list. Take a moment and look around at your present condition. Now look outside of your present condition. Just because something appears beyond arm's reach does not mean that it is unattainable. And, conversely, just because something is right next to you does not mean that you have to use it. *Now* houses everything at your disposal, whether easy or difficult to obtain.

Now is simply the square you are on at this particular juncture in the game of life. The foundational character that started your sketch shows remains. Every square in the sequence to this point remains. Those prior characters make up what you remember. The characters and every doodle on the square where you stand are within your *now*. The squares after your *now* are your projections. *Now* is the square of paper that you are drawn on. *Now* consists of your ability to do everything that you've done coupled with new variations. What you knew yesterday, you know now; however, what you learn today *governs* what you know now, what you knew from yesterday, and enables the possibilities of things not yet obtained — unless you are not paying attention to *now*. It is critically important that you make the proper distinction between remembering, projecting and being. When these lines are skewed, you cheat yourself from the complete option package of *now*. If your eyes are locked on the past or solely on the potential, parameters restrict and confine you. When you pay attention to *now*, you realize your boundaries but are not confined to them.

You've got two options. You either ignore *now* or pay attention to it. Ignoring *now* fosters an irresponsible *now*. And it stands to reason that paying attention to *now* fosters a responsible *now*. With the above analogy given it may seem to suggest that all life is predestined. It may seem that some governing other preordains our dreams for tomorrow. Under that assumption, why do anything? But that is not how the model works. It works rather to illustrate how we project, remember and exist. Anything that you see beyond the square where you now stand is your own projection of the possible. There has not been one moment of your existence when you were outside of *now*. But you've allowed either your prospects or your memories of something to dictate how you should act in a particular *now* moment. Take note of this. You are, no doubt, doing it right now. You are remembering your yesterday and contemplating your tomorrow to make a choice today. To ignore what happened or neglect the possible is to diminish your *now*. Right *now* you stand at the crossroads of making decisions — uninformed or informed. What tips the scale is allowing what is no longer or what is not yet to cloud the perception of *now*.

THE IRRESPONSIBLE NOW

The choices that you make now can be either irresponsible or responsible. The legislation of what is or is not a responsible choice depends on who you are. Yet there are similarities between every irresponsible or responsible now. The irresponsible *now* is riddled with tunnel vision, excuses, outside convincing, laziness and disregard of consequences. The converse of this is the responsible now. The responsible now is under girded by complete awareness. First let's examine the irresponsible now.

It is irresponsible, for example, to accept the ill-fated notion that nothing beyond your perception is available to you. This is tunnel vision at best. The mistaken belief that I am doomed to die miserable and alone is an example of such tunnel vision, and so is the belief that no one understands me. Break these two phrases down. The first phrase is mere projection and unfounded: no one can know whether or not you are going to encounter a person that appreciates your character. You are not actually limited to a miserable state of mind. You don't know the future. The other phrase, no one understands me, includes both what you remember and what you project. You have yet to encounter a person who you feel appreciates who you are, and you don't think that you ever will find that person. The language in these two statements makes assumptions that cannot be proved. To react to the limited perception that "I am doomed to die miserable and alone, and no one understands me" is to limit your learning potential and act irresponsibly. Neither the past nor the potential have any right to dictate your *now*. Of course, do negotiate between what you remember and what you project. But if you neglect the mediator *now*, you will forfeit growth beyond what you have already done and what you believe you will be able to do.

Similar to tunnel vision is the notion that you are entirely obligated to outside forces. When you are manipulated by the idea that you must perform a task due to the bullying of something or someone else, you are being irresponsible. Take, for example, the assumption that I have children, so my dreams have to be put on hold. Sorry. Harsh as it may sound, that's just a lame excuse that leaves you convinced by social teaching that says your greatness should be shelved because a child has to be fed. You are allowing an excuse to inhibit your best self when you won't do, don't do, or say you can't do because your parents disapprove, probability seems unlikely where you live, the money is unavailable, or your religion forbids. You are irresponsible when you declare that you are too old or too young; you are using an excuse. Any concept outside of you that presupposes the scope of your success is irresponsible. What you know and have experienced is your *now*. When you submit unconsciously to outside ideas, you accept notions that limit your *now*. *Now* provides total access to everything that you know and think. Excuses only surrender your *now* to the thinking around you. Let's say that you are a popular, positive, role model with great esteem attributed to your presence. You have great material wealth and firmly established in the community. If you have accomplished all of these attributes because of what others say about you and to you, you are being irresponsible. Coercion by social reinforcements may not embrace and support all that is you. You shouldn't care whether people say if you are good or bad. If you do things because people say to, you are using an excuse. You must know you for yourself. Excuses are irresponsible.

There are occasions for conscious irresponsibility, when you just want to be. Vacations are needful. There are times when you don't want to think about what is best for you. You want to be carried away. You want a good book, movie, or spa to take you away without a care in this world. I feel you. Done responsibly, irresponsibility is mandatory. But should you try to live in heaven every day, expect hell.

There are consequences to your actions. I don't care if it is a one-night stand. Expect consequences. If you needed a break from the day-to-day and you went out to get a quick fix, OK. Something is going to come of that quick fix. Inherent in every action is a reaction. If you believe that for every action there is a reaction, then why is it that you are neglecting to consider consequences of your actions? *Now* affords you speculative thought, emotional drive, historical records and immediate perception of what's around you. To think that some things could be done without consequence is absolute irresponsibility. If you sang a song with polished talent and conviction despite its lack of comparison to Whitney Houston's best, it will not be disregarded. If you flippantly put a derogatory comment out there for another to hear, it will be under consideration. Talking to yourself in a closet will warrant consideration. For every action there is a reaction. To neglect the consideration of consequences is to exist in the irresponsible *now*.

THE RESPONSIBLE NOW

The responsible *now* is not complicated in theory. The responsible *now* simply states: it is possible. What is possible? Anything. It is possible to be happy or sad. It is possible to succeed or fail. It is possible to be great or not so great. It is possible. The scope of the responsible *now* gives you leverage to try it all. The only inhibitor of all that you don't try is you. Because *now* allows you the possibility of doing it all.

The difficulties of the responsible *now* are laced in your beliefs and actions. When you are playing the role of the irresponsible, and you don't believe anything outside of what you believe, you stifle the possible. Your actions follow what you believe. If you don't believe beyond your influences, then you will only achieve what your influencers provide for you. But, should you open up and see all that is on the square where you stand, you will know that you *now* have the possibility to embrace new experiences. The difficulties of the responsible *now* are that it demands that you consistently open up your beliefs and change your actions.

Consistently changing for your greater good and, subsequently, everything around you is a definition for adaptability. Without individual adaptability, corporate cohesion is impossible. Life stands alone. You need sustenance for your biological continuity, but that's about all. You don't need a job, house, money, cars, clothes, friends, or anything that is involved in the game of life in order to survive. You can just exist outside of civilization. But, since you are reading this book, you probably don't live in an uncivilized world. What I am saying is that everything around us in a civilized community is just window dressing. Window dressing is not necessary for the non-game of *now*. But when you desire *now* to play the game, you have to adapt to the ever-changing rules of the game. Without adaptation you are put out of the game.

The responsible *now* knows that it is possible. If your desire, for example, is the beneficial fruits of the game, then your response has to be appropriate.

Don't tell yourself that it is the number of earth rotations that you've existed that has disallowed your success in the game. Don't tell yourself that you don't have enough time remaining to be successful in this game. Lack of success in this game is not because of your family, where you are, what you have, what you look like or any other external factor. *Now* provides the possible. Adapt to the rules of this game and go out and get what you want *now*.

The Game

A game is a competitive activity where one or more individuals aspire to achieve a designated end while adhering to the pre-established rules that govern the path to reaching that designated end. When a person establishes that he or she wants to play a particular game, they are subjecting themselves to abiding by a certain set of rules. If the objective is to win the game one has to become very astute either in ways of abiding by the rules while progressing toward the desired end, breaking the rules without penalty while progressing toward the desired end, or changing the rules while progressing toward the desired end and convincing all involved that it is the same game.

Keeping game in mind, my brother and I were discussing issues of living. With great passion he explained to me that life is no game. I agree. As a matter of fact, I would hope that everyone could understand his declaration; life is no game. As Brian, my brother, continued his oration on how he felt that I was introducing a game element to life I realized that he had become so immersed in the events of living that life was being defined as the events. It is with this definition of life that I disagree. Life is independent of and not defined by the events of living. For example, lets say that you are the "life of the party." Prior to you showing up at the party, people were not talking, dancing, exploring, in general no one was having any fun. Suddenly, you show up at the party and people begin to notice the great time they are having talking, dancing, exploring, and having fun. Two things to point out; one - prior to you getting to the party talking, dancing, exploring and fun were characteristics that existed without your presence and two - you, life, existed without those characteristics. The party does not define life yet the party is affected by life. Prior to you being introduced into this world every problem or success that you have experienced or thought about experiencing existed.

You are not defined by pre-existing successes or failures. Life is no game. There is life then there are events of living.

As a newcomer to this world of opportunity you have a choice to participate in different events of living. The events of living have their own rules, definable ends, a winner, a looser, and participants; it is a game. Your existence, to the contrary of events of living, does not have rules, definable ends or participants. You are not a game. But, you can play games. Have you heard of the terms good life or bad life? As will be discussed in the next chapter, life cannot be good or bad; life is. But a game, on the other hand, can be good or bad. A game can be good or bad because by definition there is a winner or a looser.

For fun, I picked up the board game called "The Game of LIFE." The instructions were point to fact. Put the labels on the mountains and bridge, put together and fix the spinner, buildings, mountains, and bridge to the board. Collect your life tiles and money, cards, insurance, pegs and cars. After all board pieces are fixed and game tools are doled out, the competition begins. The first person to make a play, by rule, is the person who makes the highest spin of the wheel. Within the parameters of the game there were many considerations; careers, changing careers, mid-life crisis, college, marriage, having a baby, buying a house, stocks and loans, paydays, lost of job, selling a house, cars, money etc… There were even special rules for certain careers; salesperson, entertainers, teachers, computer consultants, athletes and artists all received special treatment. The instructions were clear; in order to be a part of the game you had to abide by the rules of the game. Then, of course, there was the object of the game. The object is to "collect money and LIFE tiles, and have the highest dollar amount at the end of the game." If you have the highest dollar amount you are the winner. If you don't have the highest dollar amount then you are the loser.

I have spoken with several people about their struggles. My findings say that most people believe that they should have more stuff. Without the stuff people feel that they are unaccomplished. Or, by standards of the previously mentioned objective, they are losers. I have learned that in order to progress beyond your struggles you have to identify and separate from the game. The game is a social perception that states that everyone must at least have what someone else has, and if you have more than what someone else has then you are better. Having more is the good life and having less is the bad life. This game has such a strong hold on the world community that it has, for many, become the definition of life. If you believe in this good life bad life way, you're being duped. Scientifically speaking life is a biological manifestation. Theoretically speaking life is a spiritual manifestation. But the game has defined life as what you have or don't have as compared to others. Not so. Brian is absolutely right; Life is no game.

But a game is being played. Do you have to play the game? No. Are there huge consequences to not playing the game? Yes. Are there games within the game? Yes. Are there rules to the game? Yes. Who dictates the rules? Everyone. Who enforces the rules? Everyone. Who interprets the rules? Everyone. Can the rules be broken? Yes. Can the rules be changed? Yes. Are there consequences to breaking the rules? Yes. Can the rules be wrong? Maybe. Are the rules for everyone? Yes. Are any exempt from the rules? Yes. Can there be a new game? Absolutely.

The game is that there are rules. The only rules that have to be considered are the ones that you choose to abide by. Reconsider the chapter on socialization for a moment. In that chapter I outlined how a community governs itself by a status quo. Now you can choose to ignore the status quo and live as a nomad or you can play by the status quo rules. Living as a nomad mandates that you make up your own rules. Some people like this theory. However, living by this principle you have to accept the consequences of your actions. This is not a bad thing. But if you don't choose to honor the currency of the States, then you have to either go without purchasing goods and services from those who are adamant about sticking to the States currency standards. If it is your rule to lie, cheat, steal, kill, rape, pillage and so forth in a community that strongly disagrees with these concepts, you have to suffer through the consequences of that community. As an individual you don't have to consider time, language, money, religion or social trends. But in order to become corporate you have to play the corporate game. Humanity, in general, has accepted the need for community. Remaining a part of and becoming a part of a community requires adherence to regulatory procedures. In other words, if you want to be a part of the community, you have to play the game. In this chapter the four things that need to be identified are 1.) Whether or not you are playing a game 2.) Which game, if any, you are playing. 3.) What the game can do for you, and. 4.) If you are playing a game, how you can make the game a tool to Grow Your Greatness.

ARE YOU PLAYING A GAME?

When I was eight years old, freshly uprooted from an all black community and newly inserted into an all white community, I didn't know the rules of the new community. My older sister, Tammie, and I were sent to Knoxville Baptist Christian School (KBCS). We were the only two blacks in the entire school. While in class I would sit and observe teachers looking for the right words to describe me to other inquisitive kids asking about our differences.

Vocabulary day was always interesting; why do they say AUNTIE instead of them saying it right, ANT? Tammie would chaperon as we road public transportation from one side of town to the other, only to be berated by questions of why don't your parents bring you to school like everybody else. Every day was a challenge. Why is your hair that way? Why do you dress that way? Why do you talk that way? Can you get sunburned? I didn't seem to fit into this new community.

After each long, lonely day of school, after taking the long bus ride back across town, and after the walk home from the bus-stop, I would mope into the house and ask mama and daddy why I had to go there. My parents would console me and say to me, each in their own way, this school will make you better. I didn't get it. We had other schools available to us, with people like us. Why don't we just go to those schools? Everyday was the same thing. Tammie and I would get up early in the morning, walk to the bus-stop, catch the bus, get to school and be questioned about everything that we did.

After three years of KBCS the questions were different yet the same. Tammie and I became track stars at the school. Nobody could out run us. She was the fastest at the school and I was the second fastest in the school. So we would get questions of athleticism; how can you run so fast? The questions did not annoy me as much as they had when I first came to the school but they made me aware of me being different. I did not fit in. But, according to my parents this school would make me better. While serving my three-year sentence at the school, I began to dress the way my classmates dressed. Now I did not get different clothes, we were too poor for that, but I would arrange the clothes to mimic what was commonly being worn by other KBCS students. I adopted the same linguistic draw and speech timing as the other kids. My curious questions about the vastly different people around me faded into me accepting them as the norm and me as different. And, after each long, lonely day of school, after taking the long bus ride back across town, and after the walk home from the bus-stop, I would mope into the house and ask mama and daddy why is my hair like it is, how come I dress this way, why do I speak this way, can I get sunburned, why are we so much more athletic and why do we have to take public transportation? I didn't fit in, but I wanted to.

One of the most obvious indications that a person is prepping to play a game is when they read the instructions to the game. The instructions inform the potential players of the necessary tools, standards and timing of play. The instructions also introduce the critically important reason for play or objective. With the objective stated and parameters in place instructions make clear distinction of the winners and the losers. The only decision left to make is whether or not the game is for you. Should I or should I not play?

You can both reject the instructions and continue without variance on your chosen path or you can embrace the instructions and change to fit in.

The game begins when you willingly change to fit in. If you can honestly answer that you are not trying to fit into any structure of any concept then you are not playing a game. But, if you have altered your existence in any way to better identify with either a group or concept then you are playing a game. From a young age we have been socialized to believe that there are definite rights and wrongs. It is right to go to church, wrong to cheat in a relationship, right to help homeless, and wrong to rob banks. So when you naturally go about the business of marrying, in church, and helping the homeless while avoiding cheating on your spouse or robbing banks, you don't consider these actions as playing any kind of a game. The reality however is that you are willingly changing to fit into a set of pre-established rules. Playing a game.

The first time I got married I was definitely playing a game. I did not know it at the time; but I know it now. My Christian rearing did not afford me the liberties of premarital sex without ensuing eternal damnation. Not only was I not permitted to have premarital sex without the punishment of eternal damnation; I was not permitted to think about having premarital sex without the punishment of eternal damnation. So in order to avoid eternal damnation, by reason of fornication, I got married. I married to fit in. Fit into what, a pre-established set of rules. Another example would be when I worked as a Human Resources manager with UPS. I was taught that my attire dictated to my employees my level of authority. So the more persuasive my dress was the greater the success I would have in the corporate game. I don't like wearing ties but I wore ties to fit into a pre-established set of rules. I was playing games. Take a moment for yourself and eliminate all concepts of right and wrong. As a matter of fact make it easy for yourself and say that everything you can conceivably do is righteous activity. With this rule in place ask yourself why do you do what you do. What did you come up with? Do you do what you do because you are trying to fit into an already established set of rules?

WHICH GAME ARE YOU PLAYING?

Remember, a game is a competitive activity where one or more individuals aspire to achieve a designated end while adhering to the pre-established rules that govern the path to reaching that designated end. If, for example, you desire to be rich then you have to govern your actions according to the standards of the rich. The rules or standards of being rich are pre-established, the designated end is to become rich, and you are competing against being identified as less than rich, poor. You are playing the game of the rich. If you change for reasons of religion then you are playing a religious game. Maybe you prefer playing a business game; so you dress and talk like the corporate community. You marry to fit in; so you are playing a marital game. If you break the general definition of the game down for any aspect of your living existence you will be able to see the games that you play. There are moral or ethical standards, professional or political standards, religious or social standards, physical or mental standards, racial or sexual standards. These standards are the rules that govern their respective games. Now, please be advised, there is nothing wrong with playing games. But, when you abide by a certain set of rules, let's say the rules of the poor, while thinking you are playing the game of the rich then you will experience all of the emotions and anguish of being the looser in the game of the rich. Just because you say you are playing a certain game does not mean that you are. And, just because you say that you want to reach a certain goal does not mean that you will. The rules that you choose to abide by dictate the games that you play and ultimately the goals that you reach. If while in the middle of a football game you swing away at your tennis ball with your tennis racquet while dressed in your tennis outfit don't be surprised when you loose the football game. You identify which games you are playing when you identify your living standards. You change the games that you play when you change your standards.

WHAT THE GAME CAN DO FOR YOU.

The games that you play do a great many things for you. Your games provide distinctions of right and wrong. Your games determine if you are a leader or a follower. The games that you play dictate the people you hang around. The games you play give meaning and purpose to waking up in the morning. Other people's worth are measured by the standards of your games. Your games manage the confusions of living. Your games categorize, segment, protect, identify, exclude, invite, pronounce, and denounce.

In my late teens to mid twenties I was heavily invested in the religious game. While playing this game my constant testimony was that Jesus made me dress different, talk different, walk different, I didn't go to places I used to go, I didn't hang around the people I used to hang around, when I looked at my hands, my hands look new, when I looked at my feet, they did too, there had been a great change in me. Truth be told, I changed to fit the criteria set by my religious affiliation. I had to present myself a certain way in order to be accepted into the organization. So my appearance and those I hung around had to fit the criteria. The church that I was a part of said that it was inappropriate for women to wear pants, make-up, short hair without their heads covered, sleeveless blouses, short skirts, and any jewelry outside of weeding rings. Men were out of line if they were anything less than straight laced. A man's hair should not exceed a certain length, jewelry outside a weeding band and maybe a cross was an abomination, and a man wearing a hat inside of any building was just cause for random strikes of lightning.

Not only was my attire scripted for me by my religion but there was also protocol. Younger respected the elder, Pastor was the authority, men were the head, women were to be chase, God's people were righteous and if you were not with us then you were against us. So for me, identifying good people from bad people was easy. If they were not dressed like me, if they did not talk like me, if they did not go to church like me then they were bad people. Now, I have since then changed my game, but the point is that my game provided a service, bundled service, if you will. Righteousness, my rank and order, why I did what I did and what reward I would receive was all-inclusive in my religious packet.

In short my religious game provided me with security. Now since religion was the dominant game for me all other games were deferred to the ruling of my religious experiences and affiliations. My religion set my standards. Every person has accepted a dominant game. It makes no never-mind what game you have accepted. But understand your dominant game sets your standards. So, in times of emergencies when you have to make a right now decision without the luxury of being politically correct you rely on the truth of your standards. In the time of pressure when a decision has to be made and you are weary from the toil of the game you rely on your standards. Your dominant game sets your standard; your standards define your parameters. Your parameters house your objective. The objective tells you everything possible for you to receive by playing your game. Now, if you don't like the prospects of your objective then play a new game.

Whichever game you choose to play can be a successful tool for you if you make it so. I was taking my morning jog and saw a child running from her mother toward a friend. The overwhelming since that I received was that the child was so occupied with getting to the friend that the trip over was not a consideration. I began to reflect on my journey from where I began this morning's jog, where I intended to go and where I was in the process. Up until I saw that little girl running away from her mother and towards her friend I was desperate to stop jogging. My entire consideration was that this jogging stuff was not worth it. My knees hurt, my side hurt, and hell I've run far enough anyway. But the little girl running away from mom inspired new thinking. Is this jog only about my knees, side, and distance? No. My morning jogs have purpose. I feel more successful while running. I feel like I am doing something worthwhile when running. I feel healthier, more energized, and inspired while running. As I continued to couple all of the emotions along with the pains of jogging it began to form into this game analogy for me. The objective for the little girl was to get to her friend as fast as her little legs could carry her. The rules were run from mom to friend as fast as possible. From the moment of that little girl leaving her mom until the time she reached her friend her entire persona express one thing only. Victory. If you want to accomplish the objective of your game you have to take the good with the bad. And, just like the child running toward her friend, you have to believe that there is a worthwhile reward awaiting you. If you are going to play the game then play the game to win. Focus on your target, know what it takes to achieve your goals and without fear or reservation give all that you've got to get what you want. Life is no game but you can play the games of your choice and win.

LIFE

The concept of life has been a topic of biological and theoretical debate for some time now. The question is life spiritual, physical or both has yet to be answered. With paint-covered fingers, people across the globe smear life with anecdotal reasoning or simple constructs, leaving life dismissed as the meanderings of either evolutionary predestination or how your material wealth compares to others. I beg to differ. Life exists through the active practice of living. This active practice of living holds true biologically and theoretically. Biologically speaking, if there is not an active practice of firing synapses or responding neurotransmitters, despite the big bang, the body would cease to be. Theoretical consideration offers the same logic. If you neglect to actively pursue life, regardless of what you have obtained, you die. This chapter is devoted to the theoretical idea of firing synapses and responding neurotransmitters, the living process.

What is living? Living is the process that begins with the insemination of the possible. I told you in the introduction that I could not address what went on before you got to this earth or what will go on after you leave. That's because I don't know. And if I did know, I couldn't prove it, so all I can deal with, and—more important—all you can deal with is *now*. You may argue the role of survival, time, friends and loved ones, material possessions, religious or spiritual beliefs and any other philosophical possibility. But these ideas are intrinsic to your *now* existence. Land, air, water, physical changes, individual loss, self-doubt, confidence, love, etc., are all elements of your *now* existence. No matter what any other philosophy says, whatever your conception of reality, good or bad, this is your earth existence. Your experience, your thoughts, your beliefs, this reality, this earth, is what you've got to get on with.

Have you paid attention to your reality – the earth? Have you taken the time to see how she moves and responds to your touch? The Earth, as a willing participant in the reproductive cycle of living, is both excited and massaged by its current inhabitants. Through the loving act of copulation between mother earth and her inhabitants, the Earth shakes, quivers, and comes to the point of climactic expulsion. Earth releases her egg of possibilities and awaits the ejaculate goo consisting of intellect, emotions, and experience. Understand that at the point of your physical introduction to the Earth, you are presented with one of two choices, to penetrate the egg of life or to deny penetration. The choice is up to you. The egg of living's possibility awaits stationary in the uterine wall of growth. It is the job of you, the unbridled sperm, to seek and ferment the egg. Some find the egg quickly. Others, well, it takes a while. And yet others quit trying altogether and are washed away. A successful sperm, during the gestation period, penetrates the egg and forms the zygote. The process of living is now taking place from this conception till the bloom of adulthood.

AMNIOTIC SAC

The amniotic sac of a pregnant woman holds within it amniotic fluid, placenta, umbilical cord and the baby. The fetus is surrounded by all of the tools necessary to maintain its health. In your pre-birth period of living, you are completely dependent on what the Earth has to offer. I call it the "It is what it is period." This period of living provides food, protection and cleansing. Without question or confusion, at the beginning of living, you just try to put names to faces.

The primary tools, in this it is what it is period, are intellect and experience. This is a leaf. This is a tree. Leaves grow on trees. There are no explorations of how you feel about the leaves growing on trees or what the leaves growing on trees can do for you. You are happy with knowing the associations of the leaves to the trees and their definable characteristics. It is like when you first experience a smile from a loving face. You don't know why it makes you feel good, nor do you question the source of the gift. You just enjoy the smile. Then you log it away.

Possibility is the substance pumped into you from your surroundings. Smiles from loving faces are sources of sustenance without vouchers of purchase. Your surroundings provide free sustenance to maintain your living. This is a hard statement to make, with knowledge that there are so many neglectful surroundings operating in the world. Yet the statement is true. I don't care what your situations are; there are options of possibilities. You may not like the immediate consequences of assuming those options. But options of possibilities exist no matter the situation. Living feeds on the possibility. It is not a question of right or wrong, it just is what it is. You simply ingest the truth given to you. My boss is a racist and is impeding my success. This is not the job that I should have. It's possible to work another. This man beats me; This woman cheats on me. Everyone says that we will never be a loving couple. It's possible that you can. Statistics tells us that it's not likely to go from broke to well-to-do. On the contrary, it is possible. Possibilities lead us to believe that there is indeed reason to keep on trying to figure out the most responsible choice of the moment.

The more you consume the protein of possibility, the stronger you become. You become strong enough to move your own extremities, to enact your own thinking, and to feel what you feel. With proper nourishment, you will naturally evolve to understanding the distinguishing characteristics of existence and corporate existence. Instead of being some unidentifiable voiceless blob connected to others, you realize your own convictions. You will grow to know that both outside of and in the game of corporate existence it is beneficial to have strong bones and thick skin. Living is the process that feeds on the possibilities provided by your surroundings. The more nutrients that you take in as possibilities, the more stable you become. Then you log it away.

Other important elements of your surroundings involve your protection and comfort. The amniotic sac is filled with fluid that surrounds the baby. This fluid acts as a buffer to protect the child from bumps. The baby floats comfortably along while its transportation, the mother, is moving around like a truck, bulldozing her way over any obstacle. While mom tackles the trying situations, the baby is comfortable. You listen to the sounds of your surroundings and even name the language you speak. *No hablo espanol.* I speak English. And that's OK. You see, your community speaks English and that's good enough for you. Never mind the fact that there are a growing number of Spanish-speaking people migrating to your community. That is not your problem. You've named the language that you speak, English. Then you log it away. You put a name to what it is you should wear at particular times and places: I should wear a suit to church and a bathing suit to the beach. There are some places that expect grunge, others you should rock ice, and still others, button-ups all the way. Within each community you are safe. You don't ask questions; you just go with it. Then you log it away. At this point of living, you are unaware of the bumps and bruises being taken by your transportation, the community. You are just riding in comfort. It's nice. Skin color, politics, riches or equal rights for anything do not register on your monitor. These ideas don't mean anything to you beyond face value. Black is black. He's the president, and everybody can do anything, as far as you know. It all just is what it is. Intellect informs you that you are protected and comforted. You don't know why. With no knowledge of a corporate game, you exist as an individual. Your transportation, on the other hand, has complete knowledge of the corporate game and allows you to be comfortable in your individuality. Why? Why not? You don't know or care. You are living and loving it. You are just putting names to faces. You are comfortably protected. You don't need anything from them and don't even consider why they are taking care of you. You just take it in stride. There is no such thing as corporate existence or different existences at all because it is what it is. You just log it away.

Finally, your surroundings keep you clean. The primary cleaning assignment is given to the umbilical cord. But the amniotic fluid plays a major role as well. The two together identify and rid you of the unnecessary. With growing vocabulary from putting names to faces, you call things like you see them. Take leaves growing on a tree: You don't know it as anything else, so that's all it is. Without thought of where your waste goes or from where it comes, you just relieve yourself whenever the urge hits you. You don't even recognize waste as waste. It just is what it is. However, there is a connection between you and the mother: an umbilical cord that cleanses you of the unnecessary. This cord, through a three-blood-vessel system, ushers in oxygen and nutrients and ushers out waste. You call a drunk a drunk, no judgment, no condemnation. You say I didn't get the part. It means nothing beyond failure to get the part. That person has a lot of money. That person is without money. That family is together. That family is divided. You call a spade a spade. All of this information that is in you, you simply release. And, due to your connection to the possible, it is nothing more than a release. You have no intention to persuade anyone. You are not considering another person's perspective of self-doubt or communal obstacles. You are not defining anything as right or wrong. You're just relieving yourself of your newly-acquired categorization of characteristics. It is what it is. In this state of living, you automatically connect all things to the possible without travail of thought. You see, it is possible for the drunk to be sober, for you to get another part, for those with money to be without and those without money to be with money. It is possible for families to both be together or apart. You are connected to the possible. The possible revives you with its oxygen and nutrients and relieves you of your waste. Your complete being is without recognition of how it affects or is affected by the community in which it exists.

The amniotic fluid that surrounds you, in this pre-birth period, has to maintain a certain level or else your life will be in danger. One of the contributing factors to low amniotic fluid is that you drink the fluid. Without questioning what it is that you are drinking, why it is you have to drink, or from where the drink comes, you drink up the better part of your surroundings. Your body extracts all that is necessary for growth and continuity and designates the rest to the kidneys. If it goes to the kidneys, it is not necessary for living. Living, in this period, is not altered by what you have or don't have. You are not persuaded by your neighbor's success or lack thereof. You are not even concerned about your communal standing or rank simply because it all is what it is. So you ingest the rich and the poor, the gay and the straight, the black and otherwise, the named and unnamed and extract those things necessary for living. The rest of the cloudy issues of allocating judgment of good and bad living are sent to the kidneys. That stuff is not needful for living. It is filtered through your kidneys, sent out the umbilical cord through the placenta and filtered through the mother's kidney. Then a cleaner fluid is re-deposited back through the placenta for your consumption. This cycle is repeated continuously until birth.

This continued cycle of intake and filtering assures physical growth. Your storage bank of names to faces is strong. You can readily remember encountering certain situations. Your ability to distinguish one thing from another is uncanny. So much so, that the natural process of living introduces a new wrinkle: What does one thing have to do with the other? It is what it is, but what is it? Experience and intelligence assures awareness, but you start noticing these feelings. The natural progress of living does not allow you the comfort of being bagged and fed forever. You begin to feel cramped. You begin to feel the contracting muscles of your community requiring that you think, project, feed and feel on your own. Questions arise. You can't say that it is what it is any longer because it's actually something more. But it's OK because you know that you need something else. Then you log it away.

BIRTH

Birth marks the point in the living process when you begin to couple those experiences that were logged away with your newly-introduced emotions. Your emotions brighten the prospect of intelligence, experiences, and possibilities. You are no longer simply existing. You are feeling your existence. Something has happened. You have been slapped on your hindquarters and now you breathe a different air of understanding. The once-suitable filing system that simply placed names to faces is no longer adequate. Your storage system must be accountable for much more. It's not just the smile that affects you but rather the smile from a loving face. This concept alone introduces other people to your world. Your once-individual existence now has an emotional, corporate feel. At birth you recognize that you have not put all of the names to all of the faces. And, innately, you are aware that you have to revisit all of those names that you assigned to faces and see how they make you feel.

Finding a new emotion in the living process is like striking oil in your back yard. You become rich with new opportunities. In this period of the living process, you are not sure of what causes crying, laughing, thinking, peace, chaos, etc. But you are willing to explore. Without finger pointing, you challenge and question everything just to see how it makes you feel. Oh, it doesn't feel so good when he hits me. Wow, I was physically tired of running, but to finish the marathon gives me a greater since of accomplishment. My dog is gone for good. Why does she always sit in the front of the class? Should I only concern myself with me, or should I consider others? For nothing more than self-indulgence, you seek to understand your emotions. You are not exhausted with the process. To the contrary, the process revitalizes you. You are energized by the search to make things black and white again. You attempt to simply categorize things like you did when you put names to faces. When you encounter the most elementary aspect of sameness, you have a nourished sense of control and assume, "Hey, it's OK. I know what this is. I got this one figured out." Then, it changes.

Funny story: My little four-year-old cousin Bria was going to cheer at her first football game. As with everything that she and her older brother did, she would call her granny before going off to any event. On this particular day, Bria called her granny and was just crying her eyes out. Granny asked, "What's the matter?" Bria tearfully replied, "I don't know." Being the great granny that she is, granny talked with Bria for a while and figured out that Bria was nervous about her cheerleading debut. So granny calmed Bria and told her to do her best. Bria did great.

The living process produces responses that are confusing when first encountered. You hurt for seemingly no reason at all. There are other occasions when you have giggle fits and just can't stop. Erupting inside of you are combinations of emotions that produce physical manifestations. Everything around you seems normal. The names that you've assigned to faces appear to remain standard, but internally you are going crazy. So you call granny. Like that, in the birth state of the living process, intelligence, emotions, experiences and possibilities work in harmony. Each entity consults the other. A forum takes place. When intelligence can't figure it out, there is a historical review. If historical experiences don't reveal an answer, then the questionnaire of how it makes you feel is sent out. If that brings no satisfaction, then you explore other possibilities. The mediator, the granny of those possibilities, is conviction. Conviction is like instinct. There is no teacher, necessary validation, or drawn-out thought process that evokes conviction. Conviction knows what to do for the baby's survival. The baby is the reason for the forum. You are the reason for the forum. The forum sometimes gets confused with its surroundings and responds with, "I don't know." *You* have to apply conviction and calm the forum down. Conviction wisely encourages you to do your best. You recognize, as did Bria, that all you can do at the moment is go out and cheer.

You will find that when you do what you can do, as opposed to fretting over those things that you can't control, you will do great.

Actively working out your intent moves you closer to accomplishing your goals. Each step toward achieving your goals provides a sense of fulfillment. When you are satisfied, when you have consumed enough to live, then things come back into perspective. You are at conception all over again. Your surroundings are providing the necessary elements for living. And you are eating it up. After you strip from the forum the elements you need for living, you just send the rest to the kidneys. Then everything changes.

Emotions are like adding zeros to the end of a number. They can add infinite value. As soon as you believe that you have something figured out, it changes. The same situation produces umpteen thousand results. As you learn to walk and then run in this process of living, you become aware of a developing trend. You see similarities. You begin to project likelihood. Reason and analysis exert their dominance in your way of dealing. You're feeling your oats. Feelings inside you and things around you begin to whisper that it is not only about you. Curious whiskers of your ability to persuade someone or something else begin to surface. That once inanimate thing between your legs begins to palpitate. The living process has brought you to a new point.

PUBERTY

Oh, sugar! What is going on? It seems that with every breath that you take you are looking to inseminate or release some egg of possibility. You don't care what it is. As long as it can get you off, it's all right with you — human cause, racial cause, animal cause, food cause, religion, political, environmental, social, global, conventional, or any other possible cause you want to get into, or allow to get into you, so it can hit that spot. You've put the names to faces, and you've identified how those things make you feel. Now you want to share these brand new ideas with the world. You are going to show the world what it has been missing. And it doesn't matter how you do it. Whether in the shower by yourself, in the locker-room with friends, or in a friendly game of hide and go get it, as long as you get off, you are satisfied.

You have figured out that there are different smiles. Some people smile, but they have evil intent. Before this evil-intentioned person hurts anyone else, you seek to inform the world of the impending danger. Your mind set, in this period of the living process, is that you must tell all listeners of your newly-acquired knowledge. You are not trying to be associated with any group or cause. You are convicted. This is not some haphazard regurgitation of learned facts. You have grown beyond name-calling. It is more than naming leaves on the trees now. You feel strongly that if the trees go away, then both you and your community will lack oxygen. Your way of existence is in danger of extinction. You can't allow that to happen. You must inform the world. So you set up platforms from which to speak. And every time you see a head nodding approval, then oh, oh yea, that's it.

Your platform evolves into coalitions. With unbridled passion you seek to introduce the world to the only concept that matters. It's all about the trees. You have been made aware of the importance of sustaining certain emotions through intelligent orchestration. You don't know why this thing between your legs is so engorged, but you've just got to release it before you explode. If you could convince the uninformed world of the significance of the trees, then the world would be safe. Then one person joins your cause. Oh, yea. That's the spot. You turn on the television and see that a person of status is fighting your cause. Oh, oh my ggggo — right there, right there. More people join your cause. Yea, yea, yea, right there. You know this is right. You begin to feel your place. You know that it is about other people, but it's about you too. So, without shame, you bare your naked self. Your desires are out for all to see. You want the good life, not the bad life. You are convinced that if you have the clothes, cars, money, job, house, and popularity, then you will be able to rest from your duties of saving the uninformed world. Then, damn it, something changes.

Your body of understanding morphs noticeably. The metamorphosis is so recognizable that it's embarrassing. Without warning, in front of all of your peers, you feel the liquidized ooze of an opinion changing running down your leg. Yea, we need the trees and the leaves and all, but I would love to have a field to play in, unencumbered by the trees. What does material stuff really mean anyway? Do I need it for survival? You cramp with the notion that in some way you are bailing on your former convictions. I don't want to be a black person any more. I just want to be a person. The cramping is sporadic at first: what you should eat, what religion you should consider, should I protect animals, should I vote, are my parents crazy, are they sane, why am I hurting every month for no apparent reason? Why is the blood of change flowing? Then the cramping and the flowing becomes a normal occurrence. You foresee the sloughing off of old ideas to prepare for the new ideas. With pad in place, you catch the drip. It's not weird; it's normal. Yea, still uncomfortable, but you deal.

ADULTHOOD

When you reach adult status in the living process, you recognize what living's all about. At one point you thought that it was all about you. You grew past that. There were times when you thought life could be good or bad, contingent upon what you had or had not amassed materially. You grew past that. No longer do you allow the government of the past to dictate the actions of now. Nor are you held hostage to the meanderings of what might be. Adult status in living puts all of your influences in check. Not judging the opinions of others, you appreciate the different vantage points while maintaining your own footing. What you have grown to understand is that it's all about your adaptability. You are all grown up now. You see clearly from two main perspectives that adaptability affords: survival and desire. All that was confused before is both identified and addressed. You understand that survival speaks to your individuality. You are well aware that desire speaks to your corporate functioning. Adaptability mandates that you consume all that is around you to strip the nutrients you need to survive while getting what you desire.

Conception is *now*. Every new experience places you back in the amniotic sac. All that is around you is to maintain your living process. Embrace your embryonic state. As a fetus you are not stifled by your thinking, feeling, or projection. To the contrary, you simply react instinctively. Without instruction, contemplation, or experience, you do what is necessary to survive. While in the amniotic sac your natural process is to depend upon the fluid for comfort and protection, and drink the fluid. This world that you live in is for your survival. The well-intended people coupled with the apathetic and evil-intended people make up your social surroundings. Your surroundings are customized for you. You are enveloped in the buffering of your closest loved ones to your most feared enemy so to keep you comforted and protected. And when you long for identity, you have to ingest the nutrients of your surroundings.

Survival of your individuality is natural. Get this point. Stop and take a look at everything and everybody around you. It is all for you. Think of it this way. The only reason I wrote this book is because you are reading it. The living process teaches you that you are all things and all things are for you. Your significant other, your stuff, your past, and your potential are all for your learning. If you neglect to drink up what you have in hopes of getting new, you will die. There is no room for the new. If you believe that what you have already consumed is enough to sustain you, you will die. The nutrients have already been stripped away and all that is left is waste. On the other hand, should you choose to allow the natural process of living to take place then life will manifest itself. Your choice of living over dying will give you the ability to handle whatever comes your way. No matter the obstacles or persuasions, you will be doing what you do for the benefit of your survival and desire. You will embrace all living. Instead of being derogatory, condescending and judgmental, you will extend a courteous hand of support. The process of living enables the possible. It will be confirmed within you. You will know because you will know. As far as those around you are concerned, well, you'll hear, "Hey, do you know that young lady, or did you see that young man? Wow, what a *life*."

GROW YOUR GREATNESS

I have a common practice, a ritual that I do every morning: I tell myself to grow my greatness. Hinged subversively to this daily imploration is the notion that I have over the years permitted external forces to stunt the growth of my life's intention. In order for my greatness to grow, I must clear the path to make way for an upward stretch. What can I say? I want to let the world see the unencumbered me. So in an attempt to clear the path, I began studying people. I read books, took classes, studied religions and talked to every person who would talk with me. I wanted to find the absolute answer that would permit my best self to shine. Unfortunately, instead of finding the answer that I was looking for, I found the opposite. The questions that plagued me lead me to the understanding that most people have become slaves to existing. The regimen of day-to-day existence has muffled the greatness of most and amplified the irrelevance. Disturbing as it may sound the general populace is oblivious to the fact that they have laid aside their greatness. Why would they do this? You may ask, "Are we doing this?" But I ask you, "Are you doing this?"

One night while I was watching an animal show on television, a thought hit me. In order to survive, both animals and humans hunt. The difference between their hunting is that animals primarily hunt up close and personal. Animals have to know their own limitations, weaknesses, surroundings, and prey. Every aspect of hunting knowledge means existence or non-existence in the animal kingdom. Humans, on the other hand, have come to rely on tools, so much so that people have begun to believe that the only way to hunt or gather food is by acquiring the proper tools. We humans place more confidence in the tools than we do in ourselves.

Think about it. A person who is into fishing will ensure that the pole, casters, line, bate, and every other aspect of fishing is in place. I have known those who study the patterns of certain fish. Big mouth bass, for example, chase certain kinds of bate. Some fish are bottom feeders while other fish are jumpers. So, with the proper tools, those who fish go out and catch fish. But what happens when fishing becomes a matter of existence or non-existence for humans? What happens when there are no poles, casters, line, bate or a common fishing hole? What would you do at that time? You would fish anyway. When your existence is on the line, you prioritize accordingly. Looks and big-game purses go out the window. No longer will you fret over whether or not your shirt goes with your pants or if your teeth are white. You are not trying to impress the cameras or anyone else for that matter. You are trying to survive. So, if fishing becomes diving into a torrential, bear-infested river for survival, then that is what you do.

It is time for you to realize your greatness. Beneath the layers of outside influence and the noise of confused identity rest the greatness that will change both the atmosphere and landscape of the world. Lay aside the tools for a second and recognize the master of the tools. In keeping with the fishing analogy, most fishing talents carry what is called a tackle box. This tackle box was created to carry and compartmentalize the tools. If you have lost your greatness it is because the tools have become uncontrolled, absent, or de-compartmentalized.

The tools to which I refer are emotions, intellect, the five senses (seeing, hearing, tasting, touching, and smelling), socialization, religion, past and present experiences (good or bad), perceptions, family mandates and any other relevant association. Quite often if convincing has cost you your greatness, lost or shelved it, it is mainly due to tools gone wild. Emotions have run away with you, or intellect has taken over, so you over-think everything. You can barely hear due to your perfect vision. One tool has become your fix-it-all magic wand because that tool has become most comfortable. So instead of taking the extra step to use the proper tools for the given situation, you improvise and stick with your favorites. We learn to accept imperfect, make-shift solutions after long, drawn-out labor on a problem. The fusion of misused tools and lack of awareness of self has produced a liqueur that is 110% proof. And we're slammin' 'em back. Not surprisingly, this brew has intoxicated our community and, subsequently, us. Our judgment has become so impaired that we cannot tell the difference between our tools and ourselves.

I am here to tell you that I believe in keeping my tackle box both neat and filled with the proper tools. I want the full range of emotions available. I long to be as intelligent as possible. I thank God that I can hear, taste, touch, smell and see. I love that I was raised African American in Knoxville Tennessee. I love that, along with my siblings, I was raised by Ralph and Carolyn Lee. I love that Mr. and Mrs. Lee raised us Christian as Christian can be. My experiences are wonderful kinks in the calibration of me. I love me! And now, I understand me. But it took a long time to communicate me because I was playing the role of a tool. Tools don't eat the fish for survival, nor do they need to. Neither can a tool operate without prodding from another source. A tool cannot grow your greatness. Life is the product of living. And living is when you grow your greatness. In order to Grow Your Greatness there are four things that you have to know:

1) **Who You Are.**
2) **Who You Want To Be.**
3) **Your Plan (and actively engage in your plan) That Moves You from Where You Are To Where You Want To Be.**
4) **You have to know that you Have More Faith in Your Power Source than you do in any obstacle that you face.**

Tools can assist in your greatness growth. But you effectively grow your greatness when you master the tools available to you, acquire new tools and do not allow any tools to master you.

How To Master Your Tools

The way to recognize the master of the tools is by first reestablishing the compartments in your tackle box. One of the first lessons that I can remember learning from pap-paw was: when working on a car, always return the tools to their proper places. To do that, I had to know what tools I had in hand and where they should be returned. That principle applies to our purpose here. Compartment definition is aligned through identification. From your conception there has been a consistent base beat, a constant reminder of the fact of life. That beat, however, throughout the mayhem of existence, has been drowned by the noise of tools. The noise comes from prejudice to certain styles of existence, "bad life" or "good life." The bad life means being penniless, ugly, alone, or worse, stuck with someone. We can all work a nine-to-five for less than we are worth. Existence alone is enough to gain access to the bad life. The good life, on the other hand, seems to require just being special. The good life consists of the most money, the best spouse, popularity, and the like. In order to have this good life, you need either money passed down, good looks, genius beyond compare, or other blessings. You have to be something that most others are not, in order to have the good life. Well, not so. Remember what I told you in the chapter on life. There is no good life or bad life. People attribute characteristics to different styles of living. Most, if not all, character gifts to life or death are due to confusion in the tackle box.

Consider emotion if you would. Emotions are tools that belong in the compartment of emotion. The function of this compartment is to loosen or tighten the barometer of concern for an issue. In the case of good life or bad life, emotion has applied too much torque to the bolts of substantiality. Mechanically speaking, the big-handled wrench of pride was used instead of the torque wrench of contentment. Consequently, substantiality has become dysfunctional or stripped. So people are investing more concern in the plight of others than in their own. The result, unfortunately, is to devalue one's own life and compare it to the greener pastures of others' lives. But all is not lost. Substantiality can be replaced and proper torque can be applied to balance the understanding of where each of us stands in the grand scheme of things. And what compartment regulates this? Emotion. In order to solve the problem, use the proper tools. In order to use the proper tools, especially in times of pressure, keep your compartments in order. Emotion is a compartment. Fill this compartment with all the tools of emotion: anger, peace, love, hate, joy, frustration, apathy, contentment, tolerance, longsuffering, weariness, meekness, temperance, malice, and many more. You are not emotional; rather, emotions are tools for you to use and to organize in your tackle box.

The next compartment to consider is intellect. Intellect is thought that is understood. Your level of intellect is your capacity to understand, which is due in large part to your desire to increase your understanding. Every element of thought that attempts to increase your understanding is a tool that belongs in the compartment of intellect. Perception, intuition, deduction, reason, analysis, and speculation are tools that belong in the compartment of intellect, which is designed to regulate the acceptable level of unnecessary and necessary impurities in our streams of thought. Let me explain. Take a look at the good life or bad life from the compartment of intellect's point of view. If you accept the argument that perception is nine-tenths of the law, then intellect would demand that most of the focus to success should be invested on perception. So intuitively you would create an atmosphere that allowed you to convince others of their need to show reverence to you. Deductive reasoning and speculative analysis confirm that once you get people believing that you have the good life as opposed to the bad life, you would then be treated as a member of this exclusive party. You would be the recipient of lavish gifts and unjustifiable prejudices for your membership alone. No longer will you wait in lines for restaurant seats, but you will receive red-carpet treatment to the best tables. The problem, however, with intellect is that intellect always questions. While seated at the best tables, surrounded by the most popular, secure with the most money, and accompanied with the tastiest dish on the planet, intellect asks, "Is this it?" When an answer to this question arrives, another question ensues, and so forth without end. Intellect understands that, in and of itself, it cannot appease its insatiable appetite for understanding; therefore, certain conjectures are considered to be outside the realm of responsibility of the intellectual compartment. Intellect questions the whole of your substance with no satisfactory answer, thereby concluding there must be something else. You are not intellect. Intellect is a segregated compartment in your tackle box.

Let's look at the compartment of the five senses. The five senses appear straightforward. Either you can or you can't hear, taste, touch, smell and see. A toddler visits another toddler and begins playing with the toys made available by the hosting family. When it is time to leave, the visiting toddler begins to gather all of her newly-acquired toys. Her perception is: I hear, taste, touch, smell and see them; therefore, they belong to me. This shows how sensory perceptions are numb, at best, without some other form of consideration. The five senses actually have no being without experience and memory. To prefer the good life over the bad life, from the vantage point of the five senses, is to evaluate everything from a physical perspective. The feel of mink is so much more elegant than the feel of polyester. To see and hear ocean waves crashing is more delicate than that of screeching cars and trains. The smell and taste of last week's chili does not compare to the smell of roses and taste of caviar. All of these comparisons are true. And if you are able to hear, taste, touch, smell and see, you have options to hear, taste, touch, smell and see whatever you want. Your senses are without restraint. Consider that gold, silver, and other precious ornaments are so much more valuable than everyday rocks because of our intellectual understanding of them. What are gold and silver to the senses? Gold and silver are nothing more than metals deemed precious based on memory. Diamond is a rock. But experience defines diamonds as hard to come by, precious. From a purely physical standpoint, without conceptions of grandeur, "the good life" falls flatly in line with life and the bad life levels up with life. Restrictions of senses are only preceded by perversions of other traits outside of the five senses. Thus, you are not solely five senses; five senses belong in their compartment in your tackle box.

I am trying to get you to awareness of self, separate from tools. Your body is a tool. Socialization, religion, experiences, and family mandates are just tools. Consider the afore-mentioned tools in this chapter along with the ones that are specific to you. Know this. They are your assistants to complete a task. Without animation, the tools are of no benefit. Inanimate tools lay around without purpose, thought, feelings, or substance. Inanimate tools are without humanity. But when your hand animates a tool, you give it purpose. Without you, tools are irrelevant. So why give control to irrelevance? You are in control. You have the power. You delegate what, where, when, why and how any tool should act because only you know your intention. Identify and align your tools. With every tool that you align properly, comes authority, which increases with greater compartment identification. When you can clearly identify the tools, you can then clearly recognize that you are the master of the tools.

How to Acquire New Tools

Acquiring new tools is not difficult. They come with experience, understanding, and desire. From the day each of us took our first breath, we began acquiring new tools. These first acquisitions were unconscious, however. So how can you acquire new tools consciously?

The word *conscious* is defined as being aware of one's self. Or *conscious* can be defined as being sensitive to some thing. When you feel that you have exhausted the possibilities of acquiring the proper tools to accomplish a goal, you are mistaken. You've not exhausted the possibilities; you've just become unaware of or numb to the possibilities.

Breathing, for example, is commonly taken as a sign of life. Every moment that you breathe, you are having new experiences. Because of our laziness, we box every similar situation into the category of experiences past, instead of exploring the differences of the new experiences. You have to understand that no matter how miniscule the differences are in a situation, those differences are new tools. As a pastor I sat with several couples that were on the brink of break-up. The reason for the break-up, as told by the couples, quite often was due to him or her acting just like the rest of the men or women in their pasts. After thoroughly questioning each of the couples, I came to realize that in most cases the accusing party was not seeing the partner, but all of the other partners that they were involved with in times past. Emotions would flood the conversation and right before my eyes characters would transform to new individuals. These new individuals presented new situations; therefore, it became unproductive for me to try to address the original complaint brought to me, because the couples were not seeing each other in the present moment. You cannot see the possibilities of what is by investing all of yourself into what was. New experiences reside in each breath we take. Each breath is an opportunity to gain new tools.

The catalyst to gleaning new tools from each breath is to understand the differences of each breath. I am not suggesting that you have to monitor every breath you take. But you do have to comprehend that every breath is different. Go back to what I said earlier about breathing being a sign of life. Most people believe that, should you stop breathing, your existence here will cease. Of course there are those who argue otherwise, but let's go with it. If you stop breathing, you stop living. If you stop living, there is no need for understanding. Without life, your experiences are meaningless to your existence in this atmosphere. The same would hold true if you had no comprehension of each breath. Breathing becomes meaningless, lifeless. The possibilities have been coffined and buried. So, vital to the constitution of breathing is the signature of understanding. Every breath promotes the possibility of acquiring new tools.

Just as breathing is basic to experience, desire is to understanding. You don't gain understanding unless you want to. To understand an experience is to desire to know its significance to you and yours. Questioning what is, with intent to find the truth, is a manifestation of a desire to know. One of the scriptures that I was raised on said, "And ye shall know the truth and the truth shall set you free" (John 8:32). This verse presupposes that I have a desire to be free. Knowing the truth is a by-product of my want. Questions grow and blossom into understanding from the soil of desire. When there is no desire, the issue is dead to us. But when we lust, long for, feel, wish, desire something, we gain understanding as to how to capture or accomplish that end.

Acquisitions are made by purchase with some sort of currency or barter system. We also acquire through gifts, by borrowing, finding and stealing. And when all else fails, we can even create the things that we want. In like manner, tools for growing our greatness are acquired. When you want tools and you understand that tools are possible to have, detours are nothing more than afterthoughts on the straight path to getting them. Allow your desire to mandate that you pay attention to your every experience. Note the woman watering her yard or the kid on the corner late at night. Unscrew the bulb of judgment and see what is happening around you. See if the grass indeed grows greener on the other side of the street. And, instead of classifying the owner of the yards whose grass grows and whose does not grow, try gaining understanding with this new experience. You can acquire the new tools once you desire to understand that every breath is a new experience.

How to Avoid Tools Mastering You

The way to avoid tools mastering you is by putting them in their place. Every tool existing today originates from human desire. Now, I wasn't there. But I would dare say that the very first person who went fishing did not have a fishing pole, casters, line, bate and net in tow. The first person fishing did not sit down on the bank with a picnic basket, cold suds and wait on a bite. No, that's not what happened. What happened was someone dove into the water and caught the fish, bare-handed. After a while, somebody said that there must be a better way. Suddenly, born from the desire to do it differently, the patent and subsequent production of fishing tools was among us. We created tools. Not only did we create tools, but also we created tools with parameters. Once we place tools squarely in the center of their limitations, we recognize that we dominate. We don't have to have tools. We use them because we want to.

Without you, there would be no need for a president, queen, or dignitary of any kind. Without you, we don't need corporations. Without humanity, there is no need for money, trading, religions, rules, houses, clothes or anything else that exists. I don't believe that I will ever forget the day that I walked into work and first came to the realization that my living did not have to center around my job. As a matter of fact, I realized, my job should be centered on my living. The acquisitions of jobs, religions, social environments, languages and affiliations are nothing more than tools to amplify *you*, greatness with a name. You can even change your tools upon inspiration. You don't have to continue speaking the same language; learn another one. You don't have to stay on the same job. Get another one or work for yourself. There are hundreds of religions out there for you to choose from. Take your pick. And you don't have to live where you do. Move. Of course there are consequences to all of your actions. I understand that you might not be a risk-taker. You don't need to be something that you are not. You need only to pronounce who you are.

Contrary to popular character identification, you are not the company that you work for. Oh, let me get ignorant for a second: don't believe the hype; you are not the country that you live in. Dig this; read this one carefully and don't get it twisted. You are not the color of your skin. You are not your religion or sexual persuasion. You are not the lineage of your family. You are something else. You are you, greatness with a name.

It is time for you to get up off of your do-nothing seat and identify those things that are holding you — greatness with a name — down. Unpack your emotional baggage of experiences past and fears of tomorrow and place them in the compartment of emotions. Allow your intellectual prowess to roam as far as the chain that you've linked to it. Revisit the tutors of your past and identify the social and religious lessons given. Answer the questions of how things affect you. Know why you want to eat when you are depressed. Why do you fight when you drink? Why do you drink when you are happy? Why does owning this car make you feel better than owning the other car? What you do is what you do. But asking why you do it is for your growth. Cut away the dead weight of tools. Insist on comparing the influence of the world to the truth of your convictions. Take all the tools available to you and place them squarely in the center of their limitations. By doing so you will ensure that tools will never attempt to dethrone the master, you: greatness with a name.

Have you heard this before? Do you remember being aware of your greatness? How does it feel to know that you are great? Listen to the roar of who you are. Buy the ticket and go to your own concert. Let the beat of *you* pound louder than the noise of all the stuff around you. Master your tools, acquire new tools, and stop the revolt of insurrecting tools. The only thing you can see from this point is greatness.

Somewhere from early youth to mid-twenties, I was convinced that living was being respectful to people who admonished me. I was converted to the thinking that the only reason I had the ability to perceive people's pain was so I could exploit their pain for my gain. My creative thinking and oration skills were necessary only for manipulating situations favorably to my likes and dislikes. I would use any tool within reach that would hammer home my intent.

I was one of those who put blame squarely on the shoulders of something or someone else. It couldn't be me that needed tweaking. I went by the book. When the letter of the law was changed, it meant someone else stepped out of line. There was no bend in me. If I had available to me what everybody else had, then I could do what everybody else could do. But look what I learned on my first real fishing experience. I worked the early morning shift at UPS. My manager came to me at the end of the shift and asked if I wanted to go fishing with him. I agreed. It was about 9:00am when we hit the water in his boat. I had never cast a line before or put bate on a hook, but he was patient with me. He taught me how to bate the line, cast, and where to look. The point of this story is that I was using the same tools as he was. The only difference was us. I am not exaggerating one bit when I say that on his very first cast, he pulled in an eight to nine-pound big-mouth bass. I was amazed. Not three casts later, he pulled in another fish. A couple of casts later he pulled in another, then another fish and on and on and on. Me, I did not have one nibble all day long. It was not the fisherman's tools that made the difference. It was the fisherman.

My inability to manipulate the tools available to me hindered the level of success that I desired while fishing. Since that time I have gone fishing again. I went with two of my fondest uncles, both of whom caught fish. Again, I did not get a nibble. As a matter of fact, to this day I have yet to pull a fish from the water in response to a cast of mine. But, I'm still fishing. I will never submit to the idea that I can't catch a fish. If push comes to shove, I'll dive in the water and get a fish with my bare hands before saying that I can't. My desire is to catch the big one; and I don't want to let any fish get away. I have the tools all around me to effectively Grow My Greatness. You have the tools around you to effectively Grow Your Greatness. Everything around us is because of the baby. You're the baby and this is your world. Grow Your Greatness.